RETIREMENT
AUTOPILOT

DAVID M. GLISCZYNSKI

RETIREMENT AUTOPILOT

THE FLIGHT PLAN TO BUILD, PROTECT AND PRESERVE YOUR ASSETS

Published by Advantage, Charleston, South Carolina.
Member of Advantage Media Group.

ADVANTAGE is a registered trademark and the Advantage colophon is a trademark of Advantage Media Group, Inc.

Printed in the United States of America.

ISBN: 978-1-59932-294-0
LCCN: 2012931245

This publication is designed to provide accurate and authoritative information in regard to the subject matter covered. It is sold with the understanding that the publisher is not engaged in rendering legal, accounting, or other professional services. If legal advice or other expert assistance is required, the services of a competent professional person should be sought.

Advantage Media Group is proud to be a part of the Tree Neutral® program. Tree Neutral offsets the number of trees consumed in the production and printing of this book by taking proactive steps such as planting trees in direct proportion to the number of trees used to print books. To learn more about Tree Neutral, please visit www.treeneutral.com. To learn more about Advantage's commitment to being a responsible steward of the environment, please visit www.advantagefamily.com/green

Advantage Media Group is a leading publisher of business, motivation, and self-help authors. Do you have a manuscript or book idea that you would like to have considered for publication? Please visit www.advantagefamily.com or call 1.866.775.1696

TABLE OF CONTENTS

INTRODUCTION **09**

CHAPTER 1 | A Vision **13**

CHAPTER 2 | A Few Financial Principles
and Why They're Important **21**

CHAPTER 3 | Common Investment Strategies **35**

CHAPTER 4 | Average Returns vs. Cumulative Returns **49**

CHAPTER 5 | Safer Investing **67**

CHAPTER 6 | Guaranteed Income for Life **93**

CHAPTER 7 | Other Retirement Planning **99**

CHAPTER 8 | Case Studies...................................**115**

CHAPTER 9 | Selecting a Financial Planner...........................**123**

INTRODUCTION

I'm Dave Glisczynski. I started focusing on retirement planning when I started out in the financial planning business in 1987. When I entered the business, I was selling life insurance and investments. I did retirement planning—and more—over dinner tables to families in the evenings. During the day, I worked with businesses on their pension plans and group health insurance. The market was on an upswing in the '80s and '90s, and most people were seeing their investments grow at a head-spinning rate. I always knew that people needed to plan for retirement, but folks got drunk on the market; retirement planning was easy. Everybody was making money; it wasn't a problem. The tech bubble burst in 2000, and hard on its heels came the morning of September 11, 2001, when terrorists flew planes into the World Trade Center and the Pentagon. Suddenly, added to already significant market losses, new concerns of terrorism rocked the markets.

I had an epiphany that day that made me question my business model and how I was helping my clients. Many people were asking me, "What do I do now?" They had already lost 20%, 30%, 40%, or even 50% of their money. The market correction was brutal, about a 45% drop in three years, so if a person stayed in the market, which most did, they could have lost close to half of their money. (Later I'll discuss a common misperception about recapturing that money. People think that if they lose 40% and then get a 40% return, they have earned everything back. That's not true.)

This book will show you how to invest safely and conservatively for your retirement years. It's time to eliminate the worry, and risk, that so many people faced (and continue to face) after the market downturn. You can build, protect and preserve the assets you've worked so hard to acquire.

CHAPTER 1

❧〜❧❧❧〜❧

A VISION

———————

On 9/11, I was working for an insurance/investment company. That same year I attended a professional presentation about becoming an independent advisor, a meeting limited to the top producers in the insurance/investment world. It was an eye-opener. I learned about the true downside of variable annuities, the true history of the stock market (see Figure 1-1. History of the Dow) and the real significance of compound versus average returns. I'd never heard anyone explain the market history like the speakers at that meeting. A casual look at the market over roughly the last 104 years might suggest that it's gone nowhere but up. But in reality, if you study the chart and block out the flat periods, the market didn't do as well as most people think. Compound returns versus average returns can be very misleading, as you'll see.

Becoming independent was an 180° change from the way I had previously operated, but I could see that it was a better choice for them and for me. I was convinced, after discussing the future with my wife, Jeanette, and son-in-law, Patrick Marcell, who are in the business with me, that this new way of doing business was the way to go. I saw that in working for a career company for the previous 15 years, I was limited to selling what they wanted me to sell.

It was a tough decision, changing horses in the middle of the stream. It was scary because I was comfortable. I was happy with what I was doing. But I really felt that I had to do what was best for my current and future clients, so I took the plunge.

I felt that I had to focus in one area because I couldn't do it all and still be effective. Several years later I made another change, to become an Investment Advisor Representative fiduciary. It was a good fit, because the standards laid out in the Fiduciary Oath described the way I already did business.

OUR FIDUCIARY PLEDGE

"I, the undersigned" pledge to exercise my best efforts always to act in good faith and in the best interests of my clients, and will act as a fiduciary. I will provide written disclosure in advance, of any conflicts of interests that could reasonably compromise the impartiality of my advice. Moreover, in advance, I will disclose any and all compensation I will receive as a result of the products and services I provide you, and all fees I pay to others for referring you to me for the products and services I offer you. I recognize that you rely upon me, and are compensating me, for trustworthy advice; therefore, I acknowledge that this pledge covers all the products and services provided in this engagement."

Here's an example about how important the fiduciary duty is to me. I was invited to the home office of one of the largest insurance companies in the United States. I was one of the top 50 agents in the country and they invited us all to a conference, to hear what new and improved products were coming. I was riding in the bus listening to the other attendees, also top agents, talking. What really struck me was when I heard one agent tell another, "Yeah, I'm going to stop selling product A for company XYZ because I qualified for their trip, and now I'm going to start selling Product B for company ABC instead, so I can qualify for their trip." I was thinking, "Are you listening to yourself? Are you really going to do something because of a trip? And put your clients in a product that's not right for them?" That is not being a fiduciary. I don't pay attention to trips because they're not important to me. What matters is doing what is in my clients' best interests.

DAVE SAYS...

I love the company incentives but quite frankly I don't pay attention to them. I had qualified for a trip once but I didn't know until my marketing representative called me up and said, "Oh by the way, make sure you get your information in for this trip." I said, "What trip?" Trips and other perks aren't what motivate me. If I do the right thing for my clients, ultimately I will be rewarded and I will be paid properly.

MY STRATEGY

My strategy is to help build, protect, and preserve my clients' assets, especially those who are already retired. Not only *can* you continue to build your assets in retirement, you *must*.

One thing that people approaching retirement can't afford to do is to take too much risk or too little. This is contrary to what many advisors will tell you. The usual investment strategies want you to risk too much, promising greater returns. But risk can lead to losses that you may not have time to recover from and that's not a winning strategy.

I don't march to anyone else's drum. You may be happy with your current advisor. You may attend the same church, or live in the same neighborhood, or you may even be related to them. They may have sold you your first life insurance policy and you like them. Well, I'm sorry to break this to you but "liking someone" does not mean that person is competent in the area of retirement planning. They may fall short – or just be taking their marching orders from their home office, if they are not independent. One of the best pieces of advice I can give you is to get a second opinion about your retirement portfolio. What can it hurt?

DO YOURSELF A FAVOR:

Get a second opinion about your retirement portfolio, but not from just anyone; find an advisor who is a fiduciary! Most people are taking more risk than necessary, and worse yet, are not even aware of how much risk they're actually taking. The vast majority of people that I meet through my workshops or referrals, tell me that they want 70% of their money to be safe and 30% at risk. But when we examine their portfolios, 49 out of 50 have the exact opposite scenario; 70% of their money at risk and 30% safe. When I ask them how they could be so far off in their estimates, they tell me that they were just going with what their advice-giver recommended, and had no idea how much risk they'd assumed.

OUR FAMILY BUSINESS

I didn't take the choice to change to an independent financial planner lightly. My wife had a big influence on my decision, and she supported me in the change. It took a lot of prayer and thought. My faith is definitely a compass in my life and determines how I run my business. I look at everything and basically ask WWJD – what would Jesus do? I try to run my business with that always in the back of my mind.

After becoming independent, I made some changes that would allow our office to serve our clients in the best way possible. My wife took over the health insurance side of the business, one of my daughters, Christa, assumed responsibility for long-term care insurance, and I transitioned into full-time retirement planning. I took courses and obtained more designations that would be helpful, including a CAS, Certified Annuity Specialist in order to understand the complexities of annuities. My other daughter, Alyssa Marcell, is our customer service representative. My son, Jason, and son-in-law, Patrick Marcell, are Investment Advisors Representatives who work alongside me. In addition, we have several non-family staff members who have become part of our family.

As you can see, Glisczynski & Associates is a genuine family business. The biggest advantage of working with a family business is that it brings certain ingredients to the table. We're dedicated to our clients, and our family values mean that we have stability.

When you're looking for a financial advice-giver, look for a firm that has a succession plan in place. Who will take over your retirement planning if your advice-giver retires, moves, becomes disabled or dies? You want stability with your retirement plan, and you should know who will step into your advisor's shoes.

CHAPTER 2

A FEW FINANCIAL PRINCIPLES AND WHY THEY'RE IMPORTANT

Now that you know a little about our firm and what I believe, I'd like to introduce the concept of a sideways market, and discuss some common investment mistakes people make and their fears when it comes to money.

INVESTING IN A SIDEWAYS MARKET – OPPORTUNITY OR NOT?

A sideways market is a period in which stocks trade within a narrow range, with very few changes. It's also known as a flat market, or one with horizontal price movement. See Figure 1-1.

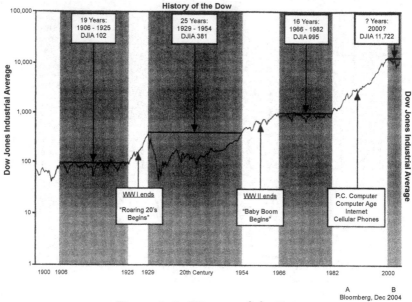

Figure 1-1. History of the Dow

If you look at the history of the stock market from 1906 to 1925, investors didn't make much money. Inflation and taxes were high. Hypothetically, if you had a dollar in the market in 1906 – not computing dividends, taxes, or capital gains – in 1925, you would still have one dollar. A person's buying power with that 1925 dollar was probably far less because of inflation and taxes, compared to its value in 1906.

How do you make money in this kind of market? The answer is simple. You buy low and sell high, but that's difficult for both the average person and the so-called "experts" to do, as a result of two things: greed and fear.

When the market is rising, we get greedy. We want some of that money. Typically people who buy when stocks rise don't see the market go up much further. In fact, more commonly, they no sooner buy then the market starts to decline. They hold on for a while and eventually say, "Oh my gosh, I'm going to lose my shirt. I'm out of here," and they sell. They don't wait until the market goes higher to sell, and they don't wait until it's lower to buy.

When the market made almost 13% from 1982 to 2003, what do you think the average investor made? Would you be surprised if I told you that it was less than 4%? It's true. Why? People acted on greed and fear. Given that very human tendency to react emotionally where money is concerned, how do you think most people can be expected to figure out how to make money in a market that is extremely volatile? They would have to know exactly when to buy and sell, which is very difficult—if not impossible—to do.

There is no definitive answer about whether investing in a sideways market is an opportunity or not. For example, if you are investing in mutual funds they're basically going to perform close to how the market does. Surprisingly, though, the vast majority of mutual funds don't beat the market index, even though they are supposed to with highly paid managers at the helm. I believe that the market is too sophisticated and fast-moving today. How much time are you going to spend watching the funds you buy or your advice-giver suggests you buy? When are you going to decide to sell? Are you going to have enough confidence to be a passive investor, and just let them go where they will? If not, you are probably not going to do very well. You are going to be stuck in a sideways market.

"LEROY AND I ARE IN THE STUCK MARKET."
Reprinted with permission, Wm Hoest Enterprises, Inc.

There have been sideways markets of 19 years (1906 – 1925), 25 years (1929 – 1954), 16 years (1966 – 1982) and 11 years since 2000. As I write, in 2012, we are in an 11-year sideways market. If you looked back 11 years from 2001, you would find similar market conditions. I don't have a crystal ball, but I believe that because of the world's current economy, and events, we are going to have a volatile market for the next seven to ten years at least (until 2019 or 2022 or longer). Based on what I've seen in my 25 years of experience following the economy, I think it will take 10-plus years for the market to really get out of the woods.

DAVE SAYS...

If you own mutual funds, ask your advisor to show you the Morningstar Report, or go on the internet to get it. This is what I call a "report card" on mutual funds which will tell you how your funds are doing in comparison to similar funds and the index. Do your homework! Always remember, past performance is no guarantee of future results!

COMMON INVESTMENT MISTAKES

As I noted earlier, among the most frequent mistakes people who are close to or in retirement make are, one, not knowing how much of their retirement is at risk, and two, having more money at risk than they should. Too often their portfolios expose them to far greater risks than are prudent at this point in their financial lives. Their only answer to why they've allowed that to happen is, "I have just been staying the course and I haven't questioned it." People need to start questioning what they are in and how much risk they really have. I am finding that the vast majority of people just don't understand the risk, nor are they aware that they can make reasonable returns without taking on added risk. Staying in pace with inflation and taxes is a must!

Another mistake is not taking ownership of their assets — assuming not one iota of responsibility. Most people don't have any idea about the risk level of a particular fund or product. They rely too much on past performance and usually buy and sell at the wrong time and too often based on hype and emotion.

People are often not getting enough information about what they are buying, so they don't know what to expect. They listen to the fund representative who is telling them, "This fund had an 8% average return in the last 10 years." So what do they expect to get? 8%. But the reality is, as we always have to say in our industry, past performance is no guarantee of future results.

We're still in the hangover stage from 1982 to 2000, when people got drunk on market returns. We still think this market is going to improve – but unfortunately that probably won't be in the near future. 2000 through 2010 is often called the "lost decade" because the S&P lost about 10% during that time. You cannot be a passive investor today. I've learned that you have to hand the decisions off to the professionals to manage your money (more on this later).

FEARS ABOUT INVESTING

One of people's greatest fears is outliving their money, and it's understandable. One survey recently said that people are more afraid of outliving their money than they are of dying. It's true; statistically Americans are living longer. Thus, in their retirement planning, they'll need to compensate for inflation and taxes, or they're going to lose ground. People are also afraid of losing all their money before they even get to retirement. Americans can best navigate the market today by leaving it to the professionals. Leave the research and the decisions about when to buy and sell in their hands. I'm not talking about money managers of mutual funds, but professionals in a research company designed to match certain mutual funds with risk tolerance, and to pursue certain objectives such as growth or inflationary funds. They should educate themselves and take responsibility for their retirement.

A common mistake people make when planning is in assuming that they're going to be in a lower tax bracket in retirement. That rarely happens. Often in retirement, you don't have the tax write-offs, and with more free time, you may spend more. I bring experts, such as tax professionals, to the table to help with these subjects. Don't go it alone; you need an accountant/CPA now more than ever, not a computer tax program or someone who just plugs in the numbers! Good tax planning is critical, both before and during retirement. You and your tax planner need to be proactive.

There are many legal tax strategies that you can use to shrink your tax bite. An often missed but simple strategy is to double up on deductions in one year for two years, compute your real estate taxes and pay twice in one year for both years, and do the same thing with your church contributions. The best tax strategies are the ones that experts suggest to fit your specific situation.

Inflation can be a real problem in retirement. Most people just don't pay enough attention to it. They're happy with a 3%, 4% or 5% return and they think they are doing all right – but in reality, they may be going backwards. If you've got a percentage of your money at risk in retirement, it is critical to make a higher rate of return on that percentage to compensate for the risk. With whatever is at risk, I am looking to hit a homerun. I'm going to be aggressive; I'm not looking for moderate risk. Just as importantly, I am also not going to be afraid to take profits when there is an upswing.

The worst thing you can do is panic. When people ask me when is the best time is to take their money out of the market and put it in safer money, especially if they are out of balance, I tell them the time is now. You don't need all the gains if you don't have high losses. If you achieve about one-third of the gains when the market goes up and don't lose anything when it goes down, you've done extremely well. I always say, "A zero is your hero."

DAVE SAYS...

The best way to navigate the market is to leave it to the professionals. As I mentioned earlier, I believe we have to use managed money. You should relinquish the responsibility for doing all that highly technical research and risk management ourselves, and leave the choices of when to buy and when to sell in the hands of experts. Readers need to understand that I am talking about a set of professionals in a research company whose job it is to match certain funds with risk tolerance and specific objectives, such as growth funds or inflationary funds. These managed models may include a wide variety of investment vehicles, ETFs, stocks, etc., not just mutual funds. Knowing when to hand off the job to an expert is part of being financially prudent. Let them do what they do best, on your behalf.

The fact is you don't need all the gains if you don't have any losses. You only need a little more than one third of the gains of the market if you don't participate in the losses. Does that surprise you? If you get just one-third of the gains in the market when it goes up, but you don't lose anything when the market goes down, you get a zero – and a zero is your hero.

I've had people tell me they're willing to risk 30% until I show them how indexed strategies can make them as much or more money without the risk. The "index" strategy is one of the missing asset classes in most people's portfolios. Many investors I speak with are concerned with the notion of taking any risk at all. I discourage that attitude, however. I believe some assets should be in managed money with a higher risk.

Some investors are in danger of outliving their money because they're getting bad information – from TV, from their relatives, neighbors and even from their financial advice-giver. They're getting incorrect advice on risk tolerances and the kinds of investments that should be in their portfolio. I see the vast majority of retirement portfolios in mostly mutual funds that invest in stocks and bonds, variable annuities, and a few individual stocks or bonds.

You'll find advisors who say you should be saving at least 3% or 4% of your income for retirement. You can't use the same percentage for everyone; you have to work backwards, beginning with the person's current income, and then determining their risk tolerance, inflation, and other variables. Then you can start talking about an appropriate percentage. When clients ask me how they should go about saving for retirement, I talk about three buckets. I tell them the majority of their savings should be in the 401(k)/IRA bucket, the next-highest amount should be in the non-IRA bucket (non-qualified bucket), and the rest should be in the Roth IRA bucket.

But I'm getting ahead of myself in talking about managed money. Let's look at risk in general.

DAVE SAYS...

The key to good financial planning is keeping your plan updated. Literally, you have to redo it every year; redo all your numbers, redo all your projections, adjust for factors like inflation or taxes, and then project out again. Adjust your target as you get closer to your retirement date.

RISK VS. RETURN

Most people believe that they have to take huge risks with their money in order to make money. That's simply not true today. Before the introduction of index products, your only choice was taking additional risk in order to keep up with inflation and taxes. But with the index products that are out there today, investors can earn reasonable rates of return, between 4% and 7%. No one needs to take high risks to achieve a good return on their portfolio. Remember: "It's not what you make, it's what you keep."

Will Rogers said:

"I'M MORE CONCERNED ABOUT THE RETURN *OF* MY MONEY THAN THE RETURN *ON* MY MONEY."

Think like Will Rogers!

It's easier to make money when you don't lose money, because as soon as you lose money, you have to make even more to make up for what you lost. If you are 10 to 15 years away from retirement, you need to start getting your ducks in a row so that you don't have too much at risk when you're ready to retire. There is not enough education within the industry about getting people to cut back on the risk as they get closer to retirement. I continue to meet people who are in their 60s and 70s with too much at risk. That's rarely a good idea.

I'm a fan of the formula known as "The Rule of 100" for determining how much of your retirement assets should be in risky investments. It is quite simple. Take your current age and subtract it from 100. Let's use a 60-year-old as an example. 100-60 = 40. That means 40% of your retirement assets can prudently be at risk. Any more than that may be too high of a percentage. You need to rebalance your portfolio every year. This is not written in stone but it's a great place to begin when you start planning.

DETERMINING THE DESIRED PERCENTAGE OF ASSETS IN RISKIER INVESTMENTS

Formula: 100 - (Your age) = Answer
Example: 100-70=30%

CHAPTER 3

—◦◦◦◦—

COMMON INVESTMENT STRATEGIES

In this chapter we'll discuss passive mutual funds and managed money, the truth about returns, and holding and folding investments. You may think these are dry topics – but just wait until you hit a financial snag involving one of these. *Then* it will be fascinating, I assure you!

CHOOSING PASSIVE MUTUAL FUNDS

Passive mutual funds are mutual funds you purchase and let sit. In other words, you buy and hold; you don't set a sell point. You say, "Okay, I'm going to invest $10,000 in this XYZ fund and when it hits $12,000, I'll sell the $2,000 profit." Or maybe, because you have held the risk investments for a while waiting for a "come back" you plan to sell $6,000 when it hits $12,000. You are hoping someone is going to tell you the best time to sell it. But no one is going to tell you, unless you have discussed it with your financial advice-giver. I have asked for a show of hands at my seminars to the question, "How many people in this room own mutual funds?" Can you guess how many hands go up? Almost all of them.

Next, I ask, "So your advice-giver has apparently told you when you are going to sell, right?" I have not had one hand go up yet. What they're doing is not so much buying and holding as buying and praying – praying that someone, or something, will tell them when that "right" moment to sell has arrived. Well, when is that right moment?

That question addresses what I see as the biggest fallacy in our industry today, which is what managed money takes away from you when you sell your managed money holdings. In my office, we still set "sell points"—something my son Jason calls "harvesting your gains." He developed a system for our office that allows us to watch our managed money portfolios with "sell points." Passive investing might have worked in the '80s and '90s (honestly, you could have thrown darts at the *Wall Street Journal's* charts and made money), but that is clearly not true today.

I referred to this before, but again, you need to accept the responsibility of ownership for what you have. In investing for retirement, you are making some of the most important choices you'll face in your entire life. Are you comfortable with the fact that you don't know what you bought, and don't understand how it works? Doesn't that seem a little strange to you? It should. If you are putting all of your faith into your advice-giver because you go to church with him, or he's your neighbor and a nice guy, that's just being irresponsible.

You can do two things on your own. One, you can go online to MSN.com and type in the ticker number (a five-letter symbol of your fund). Then compare that value to the S&P. You will be surprised to discover that most of your funds don't beat it. Two, you can get *Morningstar Reports*, a third-party rating service that collects data and analyzes your fund. If you have a large-cap value fund, for example, you will learn that there are 560 funds like yours. Then you can get the performance of the average fund and the index, and the figures for your fund. You want to beat both, but that's rare.

CHOOSING MANAGED MONEY

By "managed money," I mean investing your money with a qualified investment professional for an annual fee. The professional and his or her firm researches investments for clients, decides what to invest in and manages it.

DAVE SAYS...

Perhaps I shouldn't be as vehement in saying that "buy and hold" doesn't work anymore, because it can work. In most cases, though, it doesn't, primarily for the reasons that we talked about in the previous chapter; flat markets and market volatility. My opinion is that as a rule you can't just buy and hold anymore. If you want to make money in the market, if you are not using managed money, and you own mutual funds and want to continue to own those, you must set a sell point. You need to know from day one, when that money goes into that account, when you are going to sell.

To me, managed money is the wave of the future. The research that is done on your behalf is what makes managed money different than just picking mutual funds by fund family. With managed money, you'll have access to almost the entire universe of funds, rather than just the few fund families you're probably aware of now. There is no way that an advice-giver who is licensed to sell mutual funds can know everything there is to know about more than two or three fund families – and there are thousands of fund families. You need a managed money firm to do the research work for you. The firm must meet with managers of the mutual funds, talk with them on the phone and interview them before they ever buy their fund.

With managed money, you buy funds at the lowest possible cost. Your goal is to beat funds that are similar in risk and in style. If we are charging a management fee, we have to beat the index. Otherwise you are not going to be a happy investor. But managed money models should beat the index. Past performance is no guarantee of future results, of course, but it is fairly indicative of what the future may give us.

DAVE SAYS...

When you come to me and say specifically that you want to invest in risk or managed money, I have a method for helping you determine what percentage you want to have at risk, and what degree of risk is best for you. As previously mentioned, the "Rule of 100" is important. First, there are questionnaires that the Securities Exchange Commission rules require you to complete. Second, I created a form to "home in" on getting you the right financial tools to accomplish your goal, whether it's making sure extra care is given to passing your assets to your loved ones or creating income for life.

OTHER INVESTMENT STRATEGIES

There are a few other common investment strategies you should be aware of. If you talk about the basic investment strategies that the average person uses, they include individual stocks, mutual funds, variable annuities, and bonds, which are on the risk side. If we flip over to the low-risk or no-risk side, there is cash, CDs, fixed annuities and fixed indexed annuities. There are indexed CDs as well, which would also fall under the no risk/low risk side.

Beyond that, you can get very creative. You can get into REITs (Real Estate Investment Trusts) and limited partnerships. The majority of the clients we deal with – and probably the majority of the public – invest in the ones I previously mentioned. You have to be what's called an accredited investor to get into a REIT; in other words, you have to meet certain investment criteria, including having a certain amount of liquid assets and net worth.

This chart provides an explanation of risk as it relates to investments.

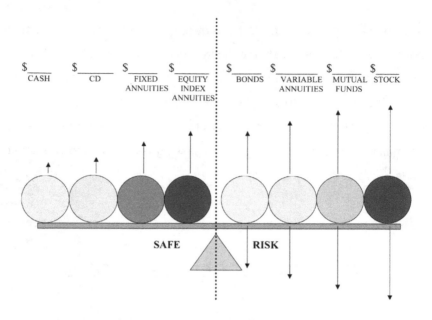

Figure 3-1. Risk Tolerance Balance Beam

I love this risk tolerance balance beam because it illustrates the two sides of investing and lets you easily visualize both of them. On the left you have your riskier investments and on the right, your safer ones.

WHY SEEKING THE GREATEST RETURN DOESN'T ALWAYS PAY

I'm going to use an example to illustrate how seeking the greatest return doesn't always pay. Let's pretend you are a potential investor and you like the market. A year ago you put $100,000 in the market and at the end of the year you have a 24% return. Now you are up to $124,000.

I ask you, "What do you say about taking $24,000 from that money and putting it into a safer investment option, and letting your $100,000 sit there and grow further?" What I would most likely hear is, "No, Dave, not right now. The market is just geared to go crazy. It's going to do well. I feel very good about it."

So I say, "All right, let's stay on it. Let's commit to coming back in a year and taking another look." A year later, you come back and say, "See, Dave? I told you. I've got $150,000 and I am up another 21%." I say, "Well, what do you think? Now we've got two years in, you are up $50,000. What do you think about taking some of that money out of there? Maybe that $50,000, or maybe less?"

"This market is still going strong. I feel very good about it."

Again I say, "All right, but let's come back in a year and take a look again about harvesting some of our gains to safety."

Another year passes, and now you are up to $193,000. You have almost doubled your money. But when I say, "Now you are up $93,000 in three years. What do you think about taking some out now? Even a little?" You say, "This thing has got more life in it. It's got legs on it. I don't want to do it yet. But let's commit to coming back in a year and looking at it again."

Another year goes by, but the news this time isn't great. "I'm sorry to tell you this, but you had a 16% drop and you are back down to $162,000. I really think we should pull some off now because I don't know if the market is going to be that strong in the next year."

"But Dave, I can't do it now. I lost money."

"But you are way ahead of the $100,000 you put in. It's $162,000." You are still saying that you want to wait. So I say, "Okay, let's wait. Come back in a year again."

Oh, man. We shouldn't have waited another year. We are now down to $133,000. Now you've got less now than you had in year two. What do we do? You say, "You know what? Let's pull the plug on this thing and move out."

Hindsight is always 20/20, but it's telling to see how many people fall into this same trap. How far ahead would you have been, had you taken your profits and reinvested them in a safe haven? You'd have ended up with more money, and avoided those losses and the roller coaster ride. Emotion tells us to hang on, when our brains should tell us to let go.

Now look at figure 3-2 in the column marked "FIA." Note that "if" we captured half the gains of our first column, but none of the losses, we have $8,387 more—but more importantly, look at the "average" return versus the "compound" return of each example.

You can get short-term Fixed Indexed Annuity contracts as short as four years. But most longer term contracts usually give a signing bonus. So if I gave you a 5% bonus, look at the difference in what it does to your return. Your return is now 8.27%, see Figure 3-2, third column. Remember, you cannot believe the average return. You have to ask about the compound return. The compound and the average are always the same when you don't have a loss. So a 5% bonus (or return) does help; it increases your return from 7.22% to 8.27%.

What about a 10% bonus? If we have $155,000 with a 10% bonus, we still have the same increases, but 9.28% and $155,000, see figure 3-2, last column. Granted, if we had known to sell at that time, we would have been better off doing that – but we didn't know.

We don't have a crystal ball, and if we're in retirement or close to it, we can't be greedy. Most of us can say we would be pretty happy with a 7% to 9% return. A 2010 report from the Wharton School of Business says acceptable returns are 4% to 7%. That's why I believe half the gains are enough, which is illustrated in Figure 3-2.

Are half the gains enough?

	Year 1	Year 2	Year 3	Year 4	Year 5	Cumulative	Average Return	Account Balance	Compound Return
Invest In Market $100,000	+24.00% $124,000	+21.00% $150,040	+29.00% $193,551	-16.00% $162,582	-18.00% $133,318	+40.00%	+8.00%	$133,318	+5.92%
FIA	+12.00% $112,000	+10.50% $123,760	+14.50% $141,705	0.00% $141,705	0.00% $141,705	+37.00%	+7.22%	$141,705	+7.22%
FIA w/5% Bonus	+12.00% $117,600	+10.50% $129,98	+14.50% $148,790	0.00% 148,790	0.00% 148,790	+37.00%	+8.27%	$148,790	+8.27%
FIA w/10% Bonus	+12.00% $123,200	+10.50% $136,136	+14.50% $155,875	0.00% $155,875	0.00% $155,875	+37.00%	+9.28%	$155,875	+9.28%

*For illustrative purposed only. Does not represent any investment or product.

Figure 3-2. Are Half the Gains Enough?
This chart is for illustrative purposes only and does not suggest a fixed indexed annuity will capture any certain amount of return.

CHOOSING SAFER, ALTERNATIVE INVESTMENTS

Mutual funds have their place, but there are other options that, surprisingly, are not widely used by most of the industry. Most people think of bonds when they hear safe money options, but 2008 –2010 certainly showed us that is not always true.

People don't understand safer, alternative investments; even advice-givers haven't taken the time to understand, or are misinformed about how they work. They end up saying, "I'm not going to do anything with that particular product. There is more profit to be made on Wall Street." There are not a lot of advice-givers flocking to insurance products or a certain market-driven product, for example, when they can make more money in other areas.

You have to know how much cash flow you have, or how much cash flow your investments are producing. You can have all the money in the world but if it is not producing cash flow, you are going nowhere and eventually all of your money will be gone.

I constantly encourage people to do their homework. Let me tell you a story about a couple I started working with in 2007. The wife was a conservative investor, but the husband was more aggressive. We were going to move about $500,000 to safety and still leave some at risk. Their broker stopped the move – even though I told them that the broker would probably do this. They decided they were going to hold off on the move, but then the wife decided to take my advice on her $100,000.

I visited with them again in 2009, and their $500,000 was now worth about $240,000. They lost half of their money. But the $100,000 the wife had in one of our safe money strategies was now worth about $115,000 even though we'd had a down year and an up year. (Chapter 4 explains how this works.)

At that point, I reiterated that I thought it was still a good idea for them to move more of their assets to less risky investments. They decided they had lost too much and they didn't want to do that, so they continued to ride out the storm. As of my visit with them in late 2010, they were still about $100,000 down from where they were in 2007. I did a quick analysis because the wife asked me to determine what they would have had, if they had taken my advice. Instead of having $400,000 of their $500,000 left, had they moved their money to the safer money strategies I had first recommended back in 2007, they would have had over $700,000 in a market that basically went nowhere. I not only would have protected their $500,000 dollars, I would have grown it by $200,000. That is the power of not losing money. You don't need to get it all, when you don't lose any.

Ask questions of your advisor if he or she is not keeping you informed. If he or she is relatively close to you in age, ask your advisor to show you his or her portfolio. I show people mine. They see what I own: I own what I recommend to my clients. Some advisors won't show you what they have because they don't buy what they sold you! So what does that tell you?

As an example I know of a person who is not licensed to sell annuities yet writes a newsletter giving advice that is mostly inaccurate, misleading or just plain wrong about fixed indexed annuities. I have written to him several times to correct him because he was totally misleading his readers. For years, I sent him basic information and said that what he was telling his audience was wrong. He wouldn't correct it. I think he didn't want to admit that he'd made a mistake. You have to be very careful about who you listen to. This person took it upon himself to offer advice despite not having all the facts.

We are in a new era, an era of self-reliance. What does that mean? You can't be dependent on Social Security. You can't depend on your kids or your neighbors. You can depend on yourself, and that's all.

DAVE SAYS...

Many advisors are great at accumulating your money, but I have not seen many who are very good at managing the distribution phase of your money. Your best defense against bad advice is to be educated. I encourage people to take every opportunity to learn more about their finances. If your current advisor isn't generous about sharing what he knows with you, and isn't willing to take the time to explain what he's doing for you, then that individual may not be the best advice-giver for you.

CHAPTER 4

AVERAGE RETURNS VS. CUMULATIVE RETURNS

There's a big difference between average returns and cumulative returns, and understanding that difference is essential to your financial health. As Ed Easterling said, in his book *Unexpected Returns*:

> *Compound returns can be far lower than simple average returns, particularly in the stock market. In fact, in the past 104 years and in 2003, the average annual return on the Dow Jones industrial average excluding dividends and transaction costs was 7.4% compared to a compound annual change of 5%. In addition, averaging the stock market*

returns over time masks the annual volatility of the market. An average number can lead to a feeling, perhaps even an expectation, of stable, consistent returns. The actual market ride, however, might more closely resemble snowboarding down an avalanche or climbing a cliff. In fact, the stock market as reflected by the Dow Jones Industrial Average has raced ahead as much as +82% in a single year and fallen as much as -34%, -53% and -23% in consecutive years. If the average moves in the market do not tell its real story, what does?

JOEL'S STORY

Let's look at Joel's story to help you understand average and compound returns. Joel, a planner who wants to retire with $1 million, is 35 years old in 1980. In his planning, Joel is working on the assumption that the stock market is averaging 10% per year. He read this in *Money* magazine and the financial newspapers. That's what everybody tells him. The truth is it hasn't averaged 10%; the facts tell us otherwise, but the media has led Joel to believe that the market did 10%. People are more motivated to put their money someplace if they think they are going to make a double-digit return.

Joel does the math and he figures that he needs to set aside $5,000 annually for the next 30 years to make his goal. Assuming that he makes that 10% in the market over 30 years, he will grow his money to $1,089,000.

Unfortunately for Joel, over time the market stops doing so well. His investments are dropping and not coming back as quickly as they dropped. Then there's the big 2001 meltdown, and other minor meltdowns follow. We talked about the lost decade from 2000 to 2010, where equities made nothing for 10 years. It turns out that during the last 10 years of Joel's plan, the markets actually ended up giving him a big goose egg.

Joel ends up with $562,000 in his retirement plan for 30 years instead of $1 million. He does the math and finds out that the actual market average return was 9.68% – very close to his 10% figure, so he is wondering what happened to his plan. He wasn't that far off in his projections about the market averages, so where's the money?

The reality is that as a result of the good returns in the good years, his balance went up. But his balances were small. Then, when his balances were larger and he had negative returns, it affected his returns much more than he expected. The real story here is that you can't believe average returns. When we are in a market that is rising and falling, you have to look at what you are really getting, not the percentage.

EXAMPLES – AVERAGE RETURNS

Let's look at some returns. Figure 4-1 shows investments A, B, C, D and E. We've got 6%, 8%, 9%, 10% and 12% average returns, respectively. Which return do you think you would choose?

Investment	Year					Cumulative Return	Years	"Average" Return	Answer
	1	2	3	4	5				
A	+6%	+6%	+6%	+6%	+6%	=30%	÷5	6%	
B	+27%	+40%	-22%	-18%	+13%	=40%	÷5	8%	
C	+25%	+45%	-28%	-21%	+24%	=45%	÷5	9%	
D	+50%	-50%	+50%	-50%	+50%	=50%	÷5	10%	
E	+27%	+40%	-50%	+13%	+30%	=60%	÷5	12%	

Figure 4-1. Five Investments and Their Returns

Investment A earns 6% per year for five years. Pretty boring, isn't it? I ask my workshop attendees, what kind of investment did they think that could be? People typically guessed that could be a Treasury or a T-bill, or it could be a bond paying a 5% yield. It could be a CD. CDs were paying 5% a number of years ago. Whatever it is, it's an investment that pays a consistent rate of return and doesn't have risk. So a boring, steady 6%. At that rate, over five years our $100,000 grew to $133,823. We are rounding up or down for this example. But let's go to something a little more exciting. We can make more money if we take more risk, right?

AVERAGE RETURNS

Investment	Year					Cumulative Return	Years	"Average" Return	Answer
	1	2	3	4	5				
A	+6%	+6%	+6%	+6%	+6%	=30%	÷5	6%	$133,823
B	+27%	+40%	-22%	-18%	+13%	=40%	÷5	8%	
C	+25%	+45%	-28%	-21%	+24%	=45%	÷5	9%	
D	+50%	-50%	+50%	-50%	+50%	=50%	÷5	10%	
E	+27%	+40%	-50%	+13%	+30%	=60%	÷5	12%	

*For illustrative purposed only. Does not represent any investment or product.

Figure 4-2. Investment A

With investment B, we've got +27%, +40%, -22%, -18% and +13%. If we add and subtract numbers, we have a cumulative return of 40%. 40% divided by the five years means we had an 8% average return. But that investment, with risk and an 8% return on our $100,000, means we made $128,505. Do you really want investment B? No, not really.

AVERAGE RETURNS

Investment	Year					Cumulative Return	Years	"Average" Return	Answer
	1	2	3	4	5				
A	+6%	+6%	+6%	+6%	+6%	=30%	+5	6%	$133,823
B	+27%	+40%	-22%	-18%	+13%	=40%	+5	8%	$128,505
C	+25%	+45%	-28%	-21%	+24%	=45%	+5	9%	
D	+50%	-50%	+50%	-50%	+50%	=50%	+5	10%	
E	+27%	+40%	-50%	+13%	+30%	=60%	+5	12%	

*For illustrative purposed only. Does not represent any investment or product.

Figure 4-3. Investment B

Let's look at something better yet: 9% offered by investment C. We've got to do better here. With investment C, we earn +25%, +45%, -28%, - 21% and +24%. A 45% cumulative return divided by five years is 9%. What is our answer? $127,838. I think I am going the wrong way – I did worse! But it's got to get better, right?

AVERAGE RETURNS

Investment	Year					Cumulative Return	Years	"Average" Return	Answer
	1	2	3	4	5				
A	+6%	+6%	+6%	+6%	+6%	=30%	÷5	6%	$133,823
B	+27%	+40%	-22%	-18%	+13%	=40%	÷5	8%	$128,505
C	+25%	+45%	-28%	-21%	+24%	=45%	÷5	9%	$127,838
D	+50%	-50%	+50%	-50%	+50%	=50%	÷5	10%	
E	+27%	+40%	-50%	+13%	+30%	=60%	÷5	12%	

*For illustrative purposed only. Does not represent any investment or product.

Figure 4-4. Investment C

The next one, Investment D, has got to be a good one – it's a 10% return. We've got +50%, - 50%, +50%, -50%, +50% which is a 50% return. Divided, of course, over the five years, we have a 10% average return. I grant you, that example is rather extreme because the chances of that happening in consecutive years are pretty unrealistic. We have had years where we've had a 50% drop and then a 50% return, so it's actually not too far off.

I included this example for a reason – to show that extra volatility brings extra risk. We had a 10% average return, yet we lost money! We have $84,375 left of our $100,000, so we actually lost money and had a negative return. But I didn't say we had a positive 10% because average returns don't tell the story. Compound returns do.

AVERAGE RETURNS

Investment	Year					Cumulative Return	Years	"Average" Return	Answer
	1	2	3	4	5				
A	+6%	+6%	+6%	+6%	+6%	=30%	÷5	6%	$133,823
B	+27%	+40%	-22%	-18%	+13%	=40%	÷5	8%	$128,505
C	+25%	+45%	-28%	-21%	+24%	=45%	÷5	9%	$127,838
D	+50%	-50%	+50%	-50%	+50%	=50%	÷5	10%	$84,375
E	+27%	+40%	-50%	+13%	+30%	=60%	÷5	12%	

*For illustrative purposed only. Does not represent any investment or product.

Figure 4-5. Investment D

Let's move onto investment E, which returned +27%, +40%, -50%. That -50% is just a big dead weight in the middle. Then there's +13% and +30%. That's a 12% return, but look at the $130,594 we end up with.

AVERAGE RETURNS

Investment	Year					Cumulative Return	Years	"Average" Return	Answer
	1	2	3	4	5				
A	+6%	+6%	+6%	+6%	+6%	=30%	÷5	6%	$133,823
B	+27%	+40%	-22%	-18%	+13%	=40%	÷5	8%	$128,505
C	+25%	+45%	-28%	-21%	+24%	=45%	÷5	9%	$127,838
D	+50%	-50%	+50%	-50%	+50%	=50%	÷5	10%	$84,375
E	+27%	+40%	-50%	+13%	+30%	=60%	÷5	12%	$130,594

*For illustrative purposed only. Does not represent any investment or product.

Figure 4-6. Investment E

None of the investments did better than this boring 6%.

EXAMPLES – COMPOUND RETURNS

Let's bring my 18-year-old grandson Logan into this discussion to help explain the difference between average and compound returns. At his age, he knows everything. Let's stick with our $100,000 initial investment and look at compound returns.

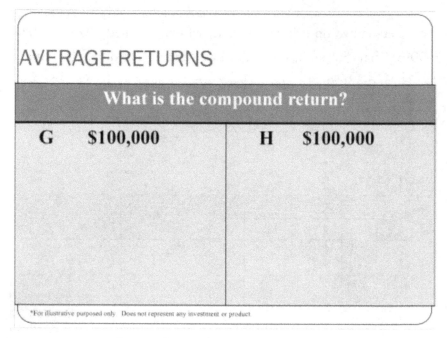

Figure 4-7. A $100,000 Investment

I asked Logan, "What is plus 30% minus 30%?" And, of course, like any 18-year-old, he said, "Zero."

Then I asked, "So that means if I had $100,000 and I added 30% and then I subtracted 30%, I should have $100,000? Is that what you are telling me?" And, of course, he said, "Yeah."

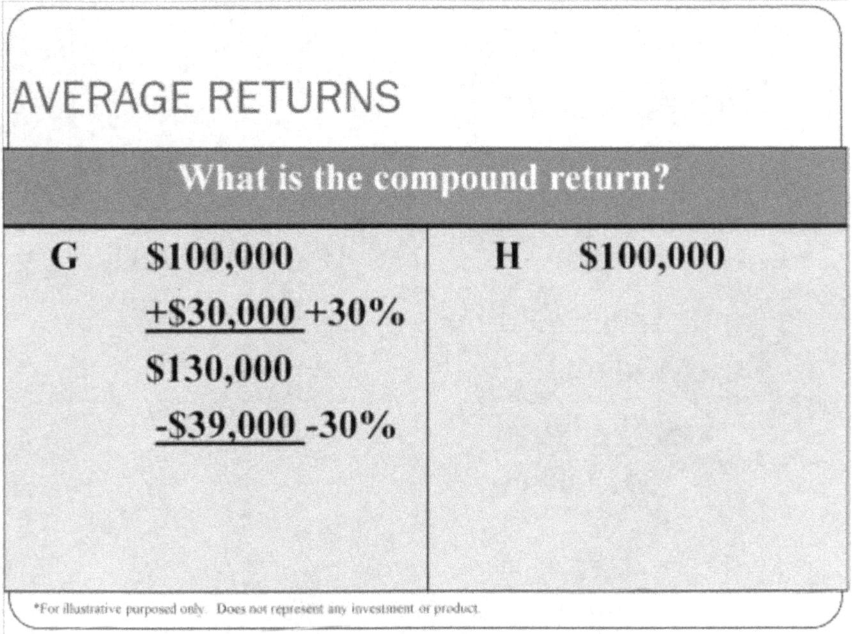

AVERAGE RETURNS

What is the compound return?

G	$100,000	H	$100,000
	+$30,000 +30%		
	$130,000		
	-$39,000 -30%		

*For illustrative purposed only. Does not represent any investment or product.

Figure 4-8. +30%, -30%

We got a piece of paper and did the math. "As you can see," I continued, "if you add 30% of $100,000, you get $130,000 – but minus 30% is $39,000, so you have $91,000. But what happened to our $100,000? I thought you said plus 30%, minus 30% was zero?"

AVERAGE RETURNS

What is the compound return?	
G $100,000 <u>+$30,000</u> +30% $130,000 <u>-$39,000</u> -30% $91,000.00	**H** $100,000

*For illustrative purposed only. Does not represent any investment or product

Logan said, "Grandpa, it must be the way you did the math. You tricked me. So let's do the minus first."

"Okay," I say, "we are going to subtract 30% and we get $70,000 and then we are going to add 30% and of course it's $21,000. But that still gets us to $91,000. So how did we lose $9,000 with plus 30%, minus 30%?"

It's in the math; it's the way math works.

AVERAGE RETURNS

What is the compound return?	
G $100,000	**H** $100,000
+$30,000 +30%	-$30,000 -30%
$130,000	$70,000
-$39,000 -30%	+$21,000 +30%
$91,000.00	$91,000.00

*For illustrative purposed only. Does not represent any investment or product.

The reason average returns are used is because they look better. The industry uses average returns instead of compound returns and I think you now know why. Using a compound return would tell the true story, because plus 30%, minus 30% is really -9%. Of course, I told Logan to go to school the next day and tell his math teacher that plus 30% minus 30% is negative 9% and he simply told me, "Grandpa, I don't need you to help me get in trouble."

Math doesn't lie. As you saw with Joel's story and with the other examples, average returns are not believable. They often mask negative returns.

EFFECTS OF TAKING INCOME
FROM A VARIABLE INVESTMENT

It's important to note that taking income from a variable investment such as the examples in this chapter is risky. Why? Because you need to earn even more to break even. Taking money from a depreciating asset compounds the problem or the injury. See Figure 4-11, which follows.

If You Lose This Much…	You'll Need to Earn This Much to Break Even:
10%	11%
20%	25%
30%	43%
40%	67%
50%	100%
60%	150%
70%	233%
80%	400%
90%	900%

Table 4-11. Gaining It Back

Referring to the chart *Gaining It Back*, if you lose 50% of your money, which happened in 2008, you need a 100% return, just to get back to where you were.

As the chart shows, people who lost 80% to 90% in the tech bubble needed a 400% to 900% return to break even. Do you see why Will Rogers also says, "When you find yourself in a hole, stop digging"? That's why, when people ask "When should I get out of a variable investment – when is a good time to leave?" I tell them, *today*. It doesn't matter where the market is, stop digging a hole.

DAVE SAYS...

Sometimes, what seems to be the best return just isn't. Don't tell me what my return is; tell me what I made. Tell me how much money I have. What you need to ask your financial advice-giver is, "What is the compound return on my investment?" Not, "What is the average return?" I promise you that if you do ask them that question, they're going to look at you with the most puzzled look you've ever seen, because they won't have any idea what you are talking about.

CHAPTER 5

SAFER INVESTING

As you probably already know, bank accounts like checking, savings, CDs, etc., are backed by the FDIC (Federal Deposit Insurance Corporation). Over the last few years the amount of the maximum coverage has changed due to the economic climate, so I recommend you either ask your banker or go to www.fdic.gov to get the most up to date number.

I also recommend you research the current amount the FDIC has in reserves to back your deposits. You need to be comfortable with that.

As for the insurance side, each state has a state guarantee insurance fund to insure a certain amount of your money or claim if the insurer you are with goes under.

History shows that if an insurance company fails, more than likely, another insurance company will buy them out.

Like understanding FDIC, you need to understand how insurance products are covered. Ask your advise-giver for the ratings of the companies they are recommending. There are many different sources on the internet available to check on the ratings of insurance companies. Research different rating companies as their reports can differ. I can't stress enough the importance of doing your homework.

Armed with this information you and your advice-giver can do a better job of diversifying and paying attention to try to not go over guaranteed limits with a bank or insurance company.

I'm not against stocks, bonds, and mutual funds, because, after all, we are Investment Advisor Representatives. I own most of these investment tools myself. Some people may have inherited stocks, or bought stock in the company they work for, and we understand that. We advise people on managed money, bonds, and stocks.

I don't follow stocks, but if a client has stocks that they like – for instance, some that they inherited and to which they have an emotional attachment – we respect that. We are very sensitive to what the client wants at the end of the day.

Before discussing safer investing, I want to be clear that every investment carries risk, even CDs. You might ask, "Dave, how can you say CDs carry risk? They're backed by FDIC insurance, as long as I'm not over the max." I'm not talking about that. I'm talking about inflation and tax risk again, which we mentioned in a previous chapter. People feel very good owning CDs and have no clue that every year inflation and taxes are eroding their principal and their buying power for the future. They can get into trouble financially by being too risk-averse, or they may not be looking at other options that are safe as well.

I believe a good rate of return for a retirement portfolio is 4% to 7%. But the bottom line is that we want a minimum rate of return that will at least keep up with inflation and taxes. Everybody wants the perfect investment that provides three things: safety, liquidity and return. What investment is there that gives you all three? It's called a dream. Nothing gives you all three.

You will always get at least one, and typically, you'll get two of the three. I'll say to clients, "I'm asking you as a person who has an interest in investing. If you could pick two of the three – safety, liquidity and return – which two would be most important to you right now?"

Most answer "safety" first and "return" second, because the notion of liquidity is mostly in our head. We think we need all this money, when we really don't. At the end of the day, what my clients want is an investment that's simple, safe, has a reasonable rate of return and potentially can keep up with inflation and taxes. They'd also like a guaranteed income for life, something like Social Security or a company pension.

Some people do throw out a number of what they think is a reasonable return; they've been well trained. There was one person who recently said "12%". I said, "I'm really sorry to tell you this, but I think we're done with our meeting. I'm not a right fit for you." And he said, "What do you mean?" I replied, "You want a reasonable return of 12%. I can't do that. Yes, I could hit it once in a while, but I'm not going to be able to give a return of 12% consistently. If that's what you're expecting from me, we're done." He quickly said, "Well, that's what I want, because I've lost so much." I said, "So if I show you a way to get out of the hole, we can talk, but understand I can't get you that." He became one of my clients.

DAVE SAYS...

When all is said and done, what matters is what you really want, what you're comfortable with. What my clients want today is simplicity, safety, a reasonable rate of return, and to keep up with inflation and taxes.

The next thing you want is a guaranteed income for life, along the lines of Social Security or a work pension. We hope Social Security will be there. Don't worry -- in my opinion, it will be. I do believe it will look a lot different for younger people, those currently under 50-55. I believe there will be less benefits and you will have to wait longer to retire and collect. So for those of you under age 50-55, when doing your retirement planning, tell your advice-giver not to count on Social Security as much.

FIXED/FIXED INDEXED ANNUITIES

Before I go on to explain the FIA, Fixed Indexed Annuity, I want to explain another type of annuity that was the foundation of the FIA. The Fixed Annuity. Some describe it as being like a CD, a bank Certificate of Deposit, but please be clear, this is for comparisons only from the point of how they work for interest crediting. A Fixed Annuity, like a CD would typically pay a fixed rate of return, say 2% per year guaranteed not to change for the next 5 years. You may be able to go to your bank and also purchase a CD at 2% for 5 years. After this comparison there are many, many differences. Each have different types of guarantees as an example in the unlikely, but possible event that the bank or insurance company goes out of business.

So how does the bank or insurance carrier determine they can afford to give you 2% per year guaranteed for 5 years? The people in charge will gather around the conference room table and set the rates based on all their analysis. You have no say or opportunity to influence or change that rate. It is what it is.

Now let's talk about the FIA, the Fixed Indexed Annuity. All FIAs that I have ever seen have a fixed account for you to put your money into instead of putting everything into an index strategy. So why does a FIA even have a fixed allocation? Well, really two reasons. First one is if you purchase a FIA that allows you to add money (note: some contracts only allow the initial premium and no contributions after issue) the insurance company will put those contributions in the fixed account to start earning the established fixed interest the day the money gets there. Then on your contract anniversary those dollars will be re-allocated to the index strategies you pick. The second reason for the fixed account is to give you an opportunity on your contract anniversary to move some or all of your money to the fixed account. Why would you do that? Let's say we are in a very volatile and precarious time. Example – the most recent of course, the real estate bubble. If your anniversary is March 15, 2008 your advice-giver says to you "I don't see good things in the markets in the next 12 months" and you whole-heartedly agree. Your advice-giver then says "why don't we move all $200,000 in your FIA to the fixed account?" then earning 3% - but your advice-giver cautions you. You are in a FIA for a reason. You want to earn more than the fixed rates out there, and the index could do very well and you could miss out on some greater index gains. You really don't feel good about the next 12 months so you say lets' move it all to the fixed. We fast forward

12 months to March of 2009. You may remember, in March 2009 we hit a low of about -58% in the S&P from the all time high. So no matter what index strategy you would have picked you would probably not have earned any index gains, you would have gotten a zero, your hero. But because you moved your $200,000 to the fixed account you were credited $6000. Now your advice-giver says on March 15, 2009, "Let's go back to the index options because we are going to reset at these very low indexes". For about 10 months, for the first time ever, I was doing exactly that for my clients. So you want to work with an advice-giver who will be monitoring this after the sale. I find when prospects come into my office who bought FIAs from another advice-giver, about 90% of the time they have never been advised to 're-allocate'. It is critical your advice-giver monitor this – ask if they do, and if they say yes, ask for at least 8-10 people you can call to verify that they have really done what they said.

Let me show you in a simplistic hypothetical chart the way a FIA works in a side-ways market. I will also show how managed money would hopefully work. This is a purely hypothetical chart. Remember, past performance is no guarantee of future results.

4 Ways to Invest Your Money

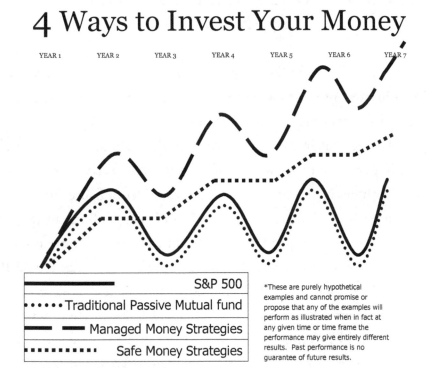

Figure 5-1.

By having a mix of safe money (indexed annuities and/or indexed CDs) along with the managed money can put your retirement on "AUTO PILOT".

Recall our discussion of average versus compound returns in Chapter 4, which used CDs in the example. One of the most attractive and safe investments is the fixed indexed annuity (FIA). Annuities have been around since the time of the Romans, but fixed indexed annuities are the new kid on the block. They were introduced in 1995.

A WORD ABOUT FIXED INDEXED ANNUITIES AND RESET

This is strictly for illustrative purposes and represents no product or company. Also, remember that annuities are backed by the claims paying ability of the issuing company.

Let me explain the concept of reset. Reset simply means that if you buy an annuity on June 1 the index will reset every year on June 1. Most indexes reset annually, but not all. Refer to figure 5-1.

In early 2011 there were about 50 different crediting methods. One of the most simplistic is called Annual Point to Point meaning the issuing company will only look at two numbers, what the S&P was on June 1 and May 31 the following year for this example.

Company ABC is using the S&P as its index though there are many available. Company ABC has a minimum guaranteed cap, the lowest your cap could go to as established in your contract. Your current cap, the most you could earn is 7% but this could change year to year, but no lower than the minimum.

You put $100,000 into a contract with Company ABC on June 1. On this date the S&P is at 1000. After one year, on May 31 the S&P is at 1100. How much did it go up? 10%. Since your current cap is 7% your $100,000 is now worth $107,000. Your contract is now locked in at $107,000.

$100,000 x 7% = $107,000

During the next year, year two, the S&P goes down to 1000. What happens to your $107,000? Nothing. It reset on your anniversary at 1000, that's important to remember. Instead of a negative you got a zero. That's why I say that "Zero is your hero".

$107,000 x 0% = $107,000

In year three, the S&P goes up 10% so now it's at 1100. Company ABC keeps the cap at 7%, Because your contract was locked in after year two you now earned 7% on $107,000. Your contract is now worth $114,490.

$107,000 x 7% = $114,490

In year four the S&P goes back down to 1000. What happens to your $114,490 now? Just like year two, Absolutely Nothing! Because it reset each year on your anniversary. Your contract was locked in.

If you had put your $100,000 in a mutual fund that followed the S&P what would you have at the end of year four? I am pretty certain you would have close to what you had started with, $100,000. With the FIA there's the power of three things working together for you, reset, no losses (you don't go backwards) and compound interest.

Some of my colleagues and I like these investments as bond replacements; bonds have a reasonable amount of safety, but again, as we know from the last market downturn, bonds can also lose money. Through default or if interest rates rise and you sell before the bond matures the bond value will be less. Also, bonds have liquidity, but you may not get all your money back if you sell at the wrong time.

Earlier I mentioned research that the Wharton School of Business conducted. The report, from 2010, discussed average returns, real returns of real bonds and real indexed annuities, and showed that indexed annuities had higher returns than bonds from 1997 to 2009. You just have to be able to deal with the time commitment. The period covered in the Wharton report is a pretty interesting chunk of time to analyze. It was a trying time for the markets, but bonds by contrast did pretty well. The study is great, and what's nice is that it's not "what if?" These are actual returns that home offices shared in the report. I can tell you from my experience that my clients have made similar returns.

That said, we can't project, we can't tell you what returns are, and we always have to give the disclaimer, "Past performance is no guarantee of future results." But when we put together a model for somebody with indexed annuities, just like stocks, bonds, mutual funds, we don't put people in one product exclusively. We will use several companies and create a laddering effect, which means the annuities mature at different times. For one client I laddered the annuities four, six, eight, ten, twelve, and fourteen years. That way, every two years after the fourth year, one of his annuities will come due, or mature. In other words, at the point of maturity, he can take all the money out of that annuity without a penalty. It gives him additional cash if he needs it. We always build in enough liquidity. The last thing I want is for one of my clients to take a penalty for getting out early.

DAVE SAYS...

My colleagues and I, who are on the safe money side, use the fixed indexed annuity as a replacement for bonds because although bonds have a reasonable amount of safety, they can also lose money, as we saw in the last market downturn. Another caveat about bonds is that you may not get all your money back if you're getting out at the wrong time. That's why I like fixed indexed products as a bond replacement.

THE BENEFIT OF FIXED INDEXED ANNUITIES OVER BONDS

Bonds will give you an interest rate, so if you buy a bond and it has a 5% yield, you'll get 5%. That's fine and good but the value of the bond can drop or rise, depending on interest rates. It's like a teeter-totter. If interest rates go down, the bond values go up, obviously, because now they're worth more. And it works the other way, too. But after the first year you can take up to 10% per year of the accumulation value out of an indexed annuity product, so you may have actually more liquidity than with a bond.

So when people say, "I don't want to tie my money up. You want me to put my money in a ten-year annuity? Are you crazy, Dave?" I ask them this question, "Let's say you have $100,000 and you give it to me to invest. I recommend you put it in a fixed indexed annuity. A disaster comes up eight months later and you suddenly need all your money. We'll say in this instance it's a 10% penalty. Most products have a similar penalty. So you're going to get $90,000 or the annuity is 90% liquid."

Now, that looks pretty harsh at first glance. But as I like to say, rather than focusing on paying a 10% penalty, focus on the good news. You have 90% of your money available to you. Is that a bad thing? You incurred a penalty because you had a calamity that you didn't anticipate. But what if you had put that same $100,000 in the market, then the market dropped like it did in 2008, and you lost 58% in March 2009? Which penalty would you rather have, the 58% loss or the 10% loss? In that scenario, you'd only be able to get $42,000 of your money, instead of $90,000. We know what the answer is. I know that there are going to be times where you might be up 20%, and you'll say, "Well, I don't have a penalty," but at least with these products, you know exactly what your penalty is. In 24 years of doing business, and the last ten focusing on the indexed products, I have not had one customer yet incur a penalty when they took my advice.

When the market went down, my clients didn't lose one cent. We call it giving them "sleep insurance." We know we can get money out if they hit one of life's icebergs, even if it means paying that 10%. But we also make sure that they have other money set aside for just those kinds of bumps.

SURRENDER CHARGES

The shortest FIA I could find at the time of this writing that I felt was a viable option was 4 years with the longest being 16 years. The longer the contract, typically the more the insurance company can give you, i.e. a bonus, capture more of index gains, etc. But the company could impose a surrender charge if you take all your money out before the end of the surrender charge period. Almost all carriers allow penalty free withdrawals of 5% to 10% after the first policy year, 10% being the most common. A few carriers will even allow penalty free withdrawals in the first year. An example would be I invest $100,000 in a 16 year contract on March 10, 2012. The company gave me a bonus of 10% so my account value was $110,000 on March 10, 2012. Let's assume I have $6,000 in index credits, which would be credited on March 10, 2013. My account balance is now $116,000. On March 11, 2013, one day into my second year, I could take a 10% penalty free withdrawal of $11,600. If you exceed the 10% allowed in my example, you could incur a penalty on the excess over the 10% penalty free amount and the issuing company could take your bonus back which is called a 'bonus recapture' on that excess amount.

While we are still on surrender charges, let's discuss a contract several companies currently offer with a return of premium feature. Here is a hypothetical example of how these work. You invest $100,000 in a 10 year contract. To keep it simple we will say there is no bonus. The surrender charge is 10% during the first 5 years. The surrender charge goes to 8% in year 6, to 6% in year 7, 4% in year 8, 2% in years 9 and 10 then there is no longer any surrender charge. Over the first 2 years you have index credits of $8,000, so your balance is $108,000. The surrender charge is 10% so $108,000 x 10% = $10,800, which would mean you would only get $97,200. Because this was a guaranteed return of premium contract, you would get $100,000, your initial premium. Now let's go out 5 years. And we will say the index credits were $30,000 so your balance is $130,000 x 10% penalty = $13,000 surrender charge you would get $117,000 since this is more than your initial premium. Of course in the 5th year you could have exercised your 10% penalty free option and got $13,000.

THE COST OF LIQUIDITY

I visit with many people who have more than they probably should in an emergency fund or liquid. I had a couple both aged 68 with $35,000 in checking earning zero, $45,000 in a money market mutual fund earning zero and $40,000 in cash in their safe at home. They had $200,000 in non-qualified (non-IRA) mutual funds and $300,000 in IRAs in a variable annuity still in the surrender period. They said to me "We really like the feeling of having more cash than we need". I asked what they felt was liquid? They said "we have $350,000". I asked them to tell me how they got to that number, I knew but I wanted them to tell me. "We have $35,000 in checking and $45,000 in a mutual fund money market, $40,000 in cash plus we have the whole $200,000 in mutual funds and $30,000 penalty free from our variable annuity". I said "Do you feel this is all liquid?" "Well of course it is, we have no backend loads on our mutual funds, the money market stays at $1.00 a share, cash is cash, checking is checking." I hated to break the news to them that they really only have $75,000 risk free from loss, the $35,000 in checking and the $40,000 in cash in their safe at home. I went on to explain that the mutual fund money market is at $1.00 a share but it is not guaranteed. What if it fell to $.95 a share? Would they sell? There have been articles and warnings that most people are unaware mutual fund money markets can go below the normal $1.00 per share constant we all tend to think will never change. I then asked what would happen if the market had a correction when they needed money? Let's say the market fell 20%. If they took money from their non-qualified mutual funds it could be selling at a 20% loss. If they took the money from the variable annuity the same problem could occur. But they said their principal is protected if the variable annuity loses money. I said yes, but not from selling low and if it dips you have to die for this company to give you your principal back. Also they were nearing 70 and would need to start taking RMDs (Required Minimum Distributions) and all the IRA money in the variable annuity was at risk. They said, "Wow, we have a problem". "Yes you do" I agreed, "and it's a doozey". I asked how they felt about paying $3,000 for the life insurance in the variable annuity. They said "we don't have any life insurance and we certainly are not paying $3,000 a year for it". I had to break the news that they were paying 1.25%

M&E charges (1% for the mortality expense (life insurance) and .25% for contract expenses). The cost of their investment accounts that are mutual funds, averaged another 1.25%. A fee for an income rider of .50% for a total of 3% a year. So in reality when their funds went up 10% they really only made 7% and worse yet, if the performance was -10% they really went -13%. "YIKES", they screamed, "No one ever told us that or at least we don't remember and are sure we would have remembered that". Nearly 9 out of 10 people who own a variable annuity that come to see me are like these folks, have no idea what they really have. I then asked them what their RMD strategy was. They said we didn't know we needed one – I explained in most cases, absolutely. With 100% of their IRA money at risk they could be forced to sell low.

Now we circled back to the whole liquidity issue. I said to them that I agreed they should have an emergency fund and adequate liquidity. But what is really enough? So I asked them when was the last time in their 68 years on this planet did they have a $100,000 emergency? "Never!" How about a $50,000 emergency? "Never!" How about a $25,000 emergency? "Never!" "So why do you think you will have one now?" "What if we have to go to the nursing home? We tried to buy long term care insurance a few years ago and were both declined. Also we don't want to tie up our money". "In a FIA if you go to a nursing home and you're still in your surrender charge period, the company will return 100% of your money penalty free including your principal, bonus if any and any earnings." Restrictions and conditions may apply. Be sure to be familiar with your contract. You could get out of your variable too but what if your account lost money, you sold low. Many companies even let you out penalty free if you are terminally ill. Some with income riders may even double your income for a period of time if you can't do as an example 2 of 6

ADLs (activities of daily living). Since they had both been declined for long-term-care this may be an opportunity to consider.

Now they wanted out of their variable annuity. But there was a 7% surrender charge. We needed to do an analysis of their income, suitability, risk tolerance etc., to determine if this was a suitable move to make. After the complete risk analysis it was determined they needed to move over $300,000 into a safer position. Their penalty on $300,000 was $21,000 ($300,000 x 7%) and giving them $279,000 to transfer to a FIA. If they could get a 10% bonus ($279,000 x 10% = $306,900) their account value and death benefit day one would be $306,900. Now I can't do justice here to explain if this couple should re-position their variable annuity into another annuity like a FIA. There are many, many things to consider. The things I already mentioned plus, what are the new surrender chargers? Do my beneficiaries get the full value or the full bonus at death or do they have to take it over a period of years, etc.? You need to further consider the appropriateness of the transfer. The new and old company ratings and other features you may or may not get. Are the surrender charges higher? Is the surrender period longer? Is there a bonus recapture etc.? Am I giving up any benefits in my old contract that the new one won't have? Replacement is very serious and you should treat it as such. Be sure you know all the facts. If in doubt, call your state Commissioner of Insurance, call both companies, basically do your homework. Replacement is not always in your best interest. Don't just move because you are $6,900 ahead. Know all the facts! Be careful!

The bottom line. More than likely you 'think' you need more liquidity than you really do. Look carefully to make sure you have enough liquid cash/money. But don't let too much or more than is needed be on vacation, sitting on a sandy beach sipping a cold drink with a little umbrella in it.

DAVE SAYS...

It's unfortunate that more advisors aren't taking this road for their clients. Advisors need to plan ahead to help their clients weather their emergencies; we make sure they have enough money, and enough liquidity. That to me is part of what it means to be a fiduciary, and why it's important that you choose an advisor who has taken that oath.

I also believe it's important, if you're going to work with somebody who's going to talk to you about annuities, that you need to work with a CAS, or Certified Annuity Specialist. Only about 1% of advisors have that designation. Now, if somebody's going to be putting a large amount of money in annuities for you, wouldn't it make sense to you that that person has had the additional education he or she needs to do the job right?

I will tell you, I've seen advisors that have been in the business as long as I have or longer who have totally misrepresented their investment products to their client. That's awful, because now the person has bought something and it's not really what they thought it was, and doesn't do what they expected it would do for them.

SELECTING FIXED INDEXED ANNUITIES (FIA)

When selecting FIAs, you want your advice-giver to pay attention not only to the companies that offer these products, but also to the product themselves. For starters, the carriers should have good ratings and not change their crediting rates significantly once you purchase. There are a lot of factors that an advice-giver needs to take into consideration; the product he/she chooses within a company has to fit the needs of the client. The most important lesson I have learned in the last decade, is the importance of working with quality carriers that not only have good rating systems, but also have good products and have consistently kept their participation solid regarding how much of the market gains in the indexes you get.

You also have to be clear about your goals. I've known people to say, "Look, I don't need this. I will probably never touch this money, Dave. I want as much as possible to go to my heirs." I'd choose a different company for that client than I would for the person that says, "In ten years, I want to buy a cottage on the lake or a motor home. I want maximum accumulation." Another client might say, "I'm looking for the maximum cash flow in retirement. I want income." Yet again, more than likely that's a different type of product.

You also want to look carefully at two-tier products. There's a chance you may not get all of your principal back if you don't follow the rules—it can take years, plus you may incur a penalty. I had a client who thought it would take ten years to get out without surrender charges, but with a two-tier arrangement, it was going to take 20. Luckily, we were able to help him get some money out, through some unique features that he was not aware of. You need a knowledgeable advice-giver to help you navigate.

It's also a good idea to explore the idea of having your premium split into more than one contract. This is important whether it is IRA or non-IRA money.

Example of IRA money – you have a 401(k) to roll over from your previous employer. It is worth $250,000. It is decided that all of this will be invested in a FIA with Company ABC. You are 55 years old and plan on retiring in 10-12 years. Who knows over that time what inflation and taxes will be. Social Security is an unknown as far as what it will provide because of the recent economic woes.

It is also determined that you want an FIA that will provide the maximum possible income and you are less concerned about the accumulation aspect. You purchase an FIA with an income rider, remember there is a fee for this rider. If we put all $250,000 into one contract, when it is time to start receiving the income the rider may spin off more than is needed. By putting $250,000 into 4 contracts, for example, you may be able to let the money in one contract start providing income, while the other contracts will continue to 'roll-up" or increase their income account. Now you may have the opportunity to start any one of the other contracts as your income needs increase. This strategy could result in greater income opportunities for you over putting all the money in a single contract. At the time of this writing I am unaware of any FIA contracts charging a policy fee - so splitting your money up doesn't make you lose a dime, but gives you potential flexibility.

THE BENEFIT OF INCOME RIDERS

Income riders can vary dramatically from company to company with differences like simple vs. compound interest rollups, minimum age requirements, maximum rollup years, waiting periods, etc. I can't emphasize enough the importance of working with a CAS (Certified Annuity Specialist), who works with FIAs full time. Let's look at a very typical example of how a FIA works when you purchase an income rider. (Remember, there usually is a fee for this rider.)

Picture two buckets. The one on your left is the S&P, or Index bucket. Many companies offer more than the S&P as an index, but for this example we'll stick with the S&P. The bucket on the right is what I like to call your funny money bucket, play money, it's not real. You put $100,000 in the FIA and, for the sake of this example, you get a 10% bonus. So from day one you have $110,000 in both your right and left buckets. Yes, I know, the right bucket is play money but stay with me on this. It will all make sense. At the end of one year the index bucket goes up by 6%. Your left bucket is now worth $116,600. Let's say the income bucket has a rollup of 7%. The right bucket is now worth $117,700.

At the end of the second year, the S&P bucket had zero index credits because the market fell but it's still worth $116,600. The income bucket still goes up the 7% "roll-up" so now you have $125,939 in your funny money bucket.

At the end of the third year your S&P bucket increased 9.39%. Your real money is now worth $127,549. The funny money bucket rolls up again by 7%, so that's now worth $134,755. Stick with me here. The clouds will part and this will all be clear very soon.

At the end of the fourth year, your S&P bucket gained 3.79%, so it's now worth $132,383 but since your funny money bucket gets a "roll-up" of 7% each year it's now worth $144,188.

You're now 65 and want to start taking your income. Though this can vary by company, typically the income will be 5.5% of your income bucket value at this age. In this example, that's $7,930 per year, guaranteed for life. Remember that anniuties are backed by the claims paying ability of the issuing company. This amount is now subtracted from the S&P bucket making that value about $124,453. But the balance in that bucket will continue to grow at whatever rate the S&P Index gives you. If the market goes nowhere, this bucket could go to zero but your income will continue for life. What if you want your spouse to get the income for their lifetime? Rather than the 5.5% payout, you may have to drop it a half-percent to 5%, depending on the company. The income would then be $7,209 guaranteed, as long as one of you is still drawing a breath. Should you not use all the money in your S&P bucket, whatever is left goes to your heirs.

Does this make sense now? Your income amount is based on the funny money value but is taken from the S&P bucket. If anything is left in that bucket after you die it goes to your heirs. Should you be fortunate and live a very long time after you start taking your income, you could end up with much more than you ever put in.

The funny money grows at the established interest rate, called the "roll-up." Advice-givers who mis-sell this call it an interest rate, but it's not an interest rate, per se; it's really a roll-up. It's funny money. It's not real. I have seen people who have bought this from other advice-givers, who come in and say, "Well, I'm making 8% interest." No, you're not. You've just got a bucket of money that is not real rolling up at 8%. It's funny money. Product features, limitations and availability may vary by state. Guarantees provided by annuities are subject to the financial strength of the issuing insurance company.

Now you'll ask, "But when I die, what happens? Where does the rest of the money go?" People often say, "I don't like annuities because it's possible I won't get all my money out if I die." This is incorrect. The only other way to get a lifetime income before income riders was with an immediate annuity where you give the company a chunk of your money. In return, they promise you lifetime income, but if you don't live long enough, you may not get it all. The company keeps it.

If you have a pension, it is essentially an immediate annuity. When you hear people say, "I've got a pension, but I don't like annuities," well, they have one; they just don't know it.

Let's use a very conservative number, $100,000, and say it grows at 4% for ten years. In your S&P bucket, your real money, is $162,826.87. But your funny money is $241,916. Now let's assume that even while you're taking money out, you're only going to average 4% return on your real money. Many companies and articles written in various magazines today don't recommend you take out more than 3%-4% of your investment due to the fact that you may live longer than your money.

SELECTING INDEXED CDS

DAVE SAYS...

There are a lot of similarities between the indexed annuities and the indexed CDs, but what counts most for both is that you can have full principal protection, and you participate in an index or a class of assets. The indexed CD is relatively new. It is not an insurance product; it is an investment product. I know, as soon as you hear investment, you normally think risk. But this is not risky, so I'm going to go over some of the basics of why, where, and when you would use an indexed CD.

If you buy an indexed annuity and you take the money out before age 59½, you'll pay the IRS a penalty of 10% on your gains.

In the state of Wisconsin, it's an additional 3.3%, so you lose 13.3% for taking it out early. There are no penalties if you are disabled or die. An indexed annuity is a fantastic tool for retirement, but you want to be careful when investing money before you're 59½.

You can use an indexed CD for retirement or you can use it prior to retirement, for people who are risk averse. It works like this: the investment objective is to use market-linked interest with principal protection. If it's market-linked, it uses indexes like the S&P, the NASDAQ, the Dow, and the Russell, or global indexes like the FTSE, the Dow Jones Euro, or the Nikkei. They can use sectors like technology, industrials, real estate, utilities, and materials. They could also use commodities, such as gold, natural gas, crude oil, energy, and basic materials, which of course are going to be affected by inflation.

Here is a hypothetical example. You purchased a 4-year CD and held that model till the end of the four years, and you were guaranteed 104% of what you put in. The topside is you could earn a higher established rate of return each year. Occasionally, the CD models will have a minimum downside risk for more upside potential. The more risk you're willing to take, the more potential.

Indexed CDs are good for somebody who's looking for a short-term investment strategy with low or no risk. If the indexed annuities did not exist, and if indexed CDs did not exist, what would you use?

DAVE SAYS...

Another good thing about indexed CDs is that the investment is not tied to your age. That makes it great for people who want to save money for college, don't want to have their nest egg for college blown away by a market correction, and want to have the potential to do better than fixed interest rates.

CHAPTER 6

GUARANTEED INCOME FOR LIFE

Let's take a quick snapshot of the current state of affairs in our country. Wall Street is incredibly volatile, and many retirees and soon-to-be retirees have seen as much as 30% of their retirement accounts disappear within the past few years. The economy remains unstable, with any real, *sustained* recovery possibly far off on the horizon. Our nation recently hit its "debt ceiling," racking up over $14 trillion in unpaid bills as of May of 2011. The future of government-backed programs such as Medicare and Social Security appears more uncertain than ever before. But what does all that *really* mean to *you*?

First, it means we're facing different times and different struggles. When our parents and grandparents retired, they likely had some personal savings. They also had the certainty of Social Security as a second leg of their retirement finances. Finally, and for many, they had a pension - or a guaranteed retirement income from their employer - that made sure they were taken care of as long as they lived.

The days of the company-sponsored pension are virtually obsolete. Couple that with the possibility that Social Security may not always be around as strong for the second leg of retirement income, and what's left *for you*? The burden of managing your retirement savings to make sure it lasts as long as you'll need it, no matter how long you live, is up to you.

Traditionally speaking, many retirees have used two primary strategies for generating additional retirement income. In "the bank way," they simply pulled interest off CDs. If you've looked at rates anytime in the past few years, you know why this approach isn't working anymore. Rates are near all-time lows. Taxes need to be paid on the gains eating up some of the meager interest.

Another strategy has been "the Wall Street way." In this approach, you would simply pull 4% from your investments each year for income purposes. The problem here? When you're *losing* money in the market, you can't just keep pulling 4% from your account without eventually depleting all the money you have.

That's why a *third* approach was developed - an approach that helps guarantee your ability to take a 5-6% payout as long as you live. The guarantees are made because of the strength of the insurance companies that are issuing the trusted product known as annuities. The Scheduled Income Payout System, or SIPS strategy combines annuity products and some strong new riders to help provide guaranteed retirement income and more tax-deferred accumulation without subjecting one dime of your hard-earned assets to the risk of the stock market. Let's take a closer look at exactly how a SIPS plan might work for you.

Based upon your *specific* financial needs and objectives, we can design a SIPS plan to help meet those needs. It's very important that this plan be *tailored* to your needs and based upon *your* particular figures because, if you're just getting someone's cookie-cutter solution, you may not be getting what's really in your best interest. In retirement terms, that means you may not be getting the *maximum amount* of retirement income you *could* be getting. One of the most common SIPS structures involves allocating money into three "buckets" to help you systematically achieve your goals.

Here's how the first bucket might work. To generate the income you need for say, the first five years of your plan, a portion of your premium would be put into an immediate solution - perhaps an immediate annuity, a series of laddered CDs or possibly a money market account. How much money would go into this "bucket" and exactly which vehicle we'll use will depend on your unique circumstances, but your first five years of income will be provided by what we accomplish here.

The second "bucket" of money in your SIPS plan is often referred to as the accumulation portion. Here, we look at solutions which build or accumulate for those first five years, while your *immediate* bucket is providing income. Then, starting in year 6 and going through year 10, this second bucket begins paying out, providing your income for this next five-year span. Again, there are a number of vehicles we might use here, but based upon your custom SIPS analysis and plan, we'll easily determine which will provide the highest income possible for that period of time.

Finally, we look at what's often thought of as the "longevity" bucket in your SIPS plan. For many, this is the most critical stage of the game - the point at which you certainly wouldn't want to be losing a dime in the market and the point at which the last thing you'd ever want to worry about is running *low on* or running *out of* income. In this "longevity" bucket, we look at products that accumulate for 10 years - while your first two buckets are providing paychecks - and then starting in year 11, we start drawing from bucket three. The beauty of this bucket? Through the use of income riders on annuity contracts, for example, this bucket will continue to provide guaranteed retirement income as long as you live. Not *diminishing* retirement income. Not income until the bucket *runs out*. Guaranteed retirement income *for life*. Guarantees, of course, rely on the financial strength of the issuing insurer.

So what does a SIPS plan really do for you? It helps take the uncertainty out of your financial future. It helps give you increased reassurance about what's ahead for you financially and helps you be prepared.

Most importantly? It lets you get to what retirement is *really* supposed to be about in the first place - enjoying what you spent a lifetime earning, taking advantage of the opportunities you finally have, *living your life* instead of wondering what's ahead. Even in the midst of these very uncertain times, you can enjoy more financial security.

Now, keep in mind, every scenario is unique. Variables including your age, your assets, your marital status, your desired standard of living - they all factor in. And the only way to ensure you're getting the *maximum* amount of retirement income is through a complimentary analysis and custom SIPS plan. Ask your advice-giver if they have the SIPS plan. If not, find one that does.

Why settle for less?

CHAPTER 7

OTHER RETIREMENT PLANNING

Retirement planning encompasses several areas: long-term care insurance, estate planning, Power of Attorney, Power of Health Care, wills, trusts, pensions, refinancing life insurance (even at 80 years of age), tax planning, Roth conversions, and reverse mortgages. We'll cover them all in this chapter.

LONG-TERM CARE INSURANCE

In my opinion, long-term care insurance is the most misunderstood and most neglected piece of retirement planning. Over the last

25-plus years of being in this business, I've seen the devastation over and over again from people who either couldn't get it or didn't want to buy it, and from new clients whose parents have been in that same boat. Long-term care insurance is *critical.*

Having long-term care insurance allows you or your spouse to continue to have a good quality of life, if you must be cared for in an assisted living facility, nursing home or even in your own home, and helps if you want to pass any of your hard-earned assets on to your children. You need to do something ahead of need, to help pay for the long-term care costs that might arise while you're still alive. Without it, your assets could be wiped out.

DAVE SAYS...

I teach continuing education, and I've taught many long-term care classes. My students share real-life stories of how catastrophic illness or accidents had wiped out the savings of their family members, every time I taught that class. Not a single class ever went by without tears being shed about the stories that were told. I could fill this book with just those stories. I can't tell you how badly it made me feel for them, and how it underlined for me the critical need to buy long-term care insurance. That's why I bought it for my wife and myself when we were both in our mid-40s.

There are several types of plans. Traditional long-term care is similar to buying car insurance, where you pay for the coverage. If you have a car accident, the insurance company pays. If you don't, all of your premiums went for naught. But you can also buy long-term care policies that have what is called a *return of premium*. So if you say, "You know what, Dave? I'm not going to ever use it, but it sure would be nice to have." That's the type you want. If you buy it at a young enough age, it is reasonable to purchase. You pay for the long-term care insurance, but then you can add a rider that says if you don't use it, your loved one gets all the premiums back at your death. In that case, you would have only lost the time and value of the money that you paid in premiums.

An asset-based long-term plan might involve putting money into a special insurance plan, generally a life insurance plan with a long-term care component. In other words, instead of buying a $100,000 CD and letting it sit there in case you need it for a nursing home, you can put the $100,000 in an asset-based contract. Based on your age, we'll say it buys you $300,000 of protection. That means the insurance company will pay out up to $300,000 if you have long-term care bills that reach that amount. But if you don't use it, your beneficiaries get the $300,000 death benefit *tax-free*.

These plans pay for assisted living and home health care, too. We can be very creative with the way we arrange them. I gave you one example in the last chapter of having $13,000 of income per year at age 65. And for no additional cost, if you get to the point at which you can no longer handle two of six specified activities of daily living (such as feeding yourself or moving from your chair to the bed and back again, etc.), you're considered disabled, and the insurance company would double that $13,000 to $26,000 for a maximum of five years.

It's very important to work with a CLTC, or Certified Long-Term Care specialist. If you need care, your spouse is only left with the house, the car, the furnishings, personal belongings and, depending on which state you live in, a portion of your total savings.

ESTATE PLANNING

Estate planning means different things to different people. Most people think it's only for the wealthy. It's not. It's the only way you have to assure distribution of all your assets to your loved ones in the most orderly and efficient manner, and to pay as little tax as possible out of that estate. I'm not an attorney and I can't give tax or legal advice, so I strongly suggest you use an attorney who specializes in estate planning and an accountant or CPA well versed in tax planning. You need a professional who is pro-active and well versed in the changing tax codes. Their services are more expensive up front, but can save you and your heirs a bundle down the road. Don't go to the guy who says, "I do divorce, I do criminal law, and oh, by the way, I do estate planning." Remember, "The bitterness of poor quality remains long after the sweetness of low price is forgotten."

You also need to know that the federal and state governments make it difficult to hide assets or give them away to qualify for Medicaid. The federal and state governments fund Medicaid and we all know the financial state they are both in.

Here's an important fact you should know about estate planning: If you have securities like stocks, bonds, or mutual funds and they're not in an IRA (because an IRA has a designated beneficiary), unless you do a TOD (Transfer on Death), you won't have a beneficiary and your mutual fund account may need to go through probate. Make sure that you do have a TOD on those. How that works depends on the state in which you live.

You must go to the courthouse and find out how to title your property, (house, car, vacation cottage, hunting land, etc.) to avoid probate. An estate planning attorney may recommend some very creative planning such as a family limited partnership. This will save your heirs time and money.

When my father-in-law passed away several years after my mother-in-law had died, my wife was put in charge of taking care of his estate by her two older brothers who had been named in the will as executors. She willingly accepted this responsibility. When he died, he had a checking and savings account on which my wife was listed as co-owner. She was able to close those accounts and get those funds without issue. But he also had a CD that was in his name only. The CD's value was just over $4,300. He neglected to put a POD (Payable upon Death) on this. It took over 18 months after his death, and over $500 in filing fees with the Clerk of Courts in the county where he died, to get that money. Since he lived in Florida at the time of his death and we live in Wisconsin, it made things more complicated. But I doubt it would have been easier if he lived in Wisconsin. The POD would have made things so much easier.

Banks don't encourage you to have TOD or POD on your accounts because it's more work for them. I've yet to hear of a bank or credit union that charged to have this paperwork done. So do your family a favor and take the time to complete the paperwork on all your checking and savings accounts and CDs.

DAVE SAYS...

I was painting my son's room a number of years ago on the Friday after Thanksgiving, catching up on chores, when the phone rang. It was a client that I'd never sold to, but whose policy I was servicing, calling me from Arizona. He'd called me at home because he wanted to know who the beneficiaries were on his life policy.

I said, "Sir, you do know it's Thanksgiving weekend. I'm not at the office. I don't know who your beneficiaries are. Call me back on Monday and I'll take care of it." He said, "No, you don't understand. I may not be here on Monday," so I said, "Where are you going to be? Where can I find you?" He said, "I will probably be dead. They've given me 24 to 48 hours to live." He couldn't remember if he'd taken his ex-wife off of his life insurance policy.

I asked him, "How long have you been divorced?"

"Twenty-one years." Twenty-one years and he hadn't checked his life policy to see if the beneficiaries were correct?

I find people are very lax about their planning until something happens. It's amazing how many times I find parents who are already deceased named as beneficiaries, or one of the children is missing from the beneficiary list, because the policyholder had a child subsequent to buying his policy and forgot to add that one on. So it's always good in your estate planning to check your beneficiaries regularly, and make sure that your list reflects your wishes.

When my brother-in-law's ex-wife died, a life insurance policy was found that still named him as a beneficiary. She had crossed him off, but that doesn't count if you don't contact the insurance company. I can't stress enough the importance of checking over all your policies, contracts and accounts every few years to be sure everything is in order.

Probate means that everything that you have is public record. When you create a trust, it can all be private. Maybe you don't care after you're dead, but most people do – they'd rather not have everybody know. So always check to be sure that your insurance products, life insurance, and annuities have a named beneficiary and not the estate as the beneficiary.

If you name the estate, it will flow through probate. For instance, let's assume that you want your assets to pass to your grandkids. Your son has two children and your daughter one child. Let's say that you're on a trip with your son, you are in a plane crash, and both you and your son pass away, but your daughter survives. If you do not have what is called *per stirpes*, your daughter gets the entire inheritance, and your son's children get nothing. Is that really what you wanted? More than likely that would not have been your intent.

Not everybody needs a trust, but they can serve unique purposes. Let's say you have four kids and one is terrible with budgeting money. You know if he got his inheritance, it'd be gone in a month or a week. You can create what's called an incentive trust, which in effect says, "When I pass, this child can only receive one dollar for every dollar he makes," or whatever number you see fit. The point of this is to give that child the incentive he needs to go out and earn money in order to get money out of the trust, and to prevent him from burning through it. Then you can set an age like 60, at which point your trust says that he can have all the money that is left. Special circumstances

RETIREMENT AUTOPILOT

can be built into the language, such as providing for money to be made available to buy a house, take care of catastrophic health issues, etc., so that child will have access if he really needs it.

A WORD ABOUT PENSIONS

If you have a company plan, you want to participate, unless that plan really has poor investments. Most pension plans have a match. I'm also talking about 401(k)s, 403(b)s and 457(b)s – these plans also usually have matches. When somebody says, "I can't afford it," go to your budget. Every time I've helped somebody with a budget, I always find ways to fund their company sponsored retirement plan.

DAVE SAYS...

Here's what I say to people who tell me, "I can't afford it." In 1988, I had a lady that came to me when I was doing enrollment at one of my group 401(k) accounts. She said, "I can't start right now. I just got divorced, I'm a single mom, and I can't afford it."

I said, "I can almost promise you that if we could fast-forward 20 years from today, you will still not be participating if we don't start now." The group was matching up to 6%, so I suggested, "Let's just start with 1%," and I calculated how much that would cost her per day. It was about the price of a Diet Coke! That was all.

So she agreed to start with 1%, and I said, "Now, when you get a raise, go to 2%. When you get a bill paid off, go to 3%."

She followed my advice, and then some. Now, twenty years later, she is putting in 20% of her paycheck, and she tells me to this day that she never would've gotten that done if she hadn't taken my advice to begin with that 1%.

"Don't eat the apple all in one bite, just nibble at it," because if you try to eat the whole apple, you'll choke. If you have a company match, it's the perfect incentive to save. Otherwise, it's like you're leaving free money on the table.

A couple in their early 60s came to see my son, Jason, to have him help them plan their rapidly approaching retirement. Along with all the other questions asked, Jason inquired, "How much have you saved so far?" They answered "Nothing, that's why we need your help." How much do you think Jason could do for them? Nothing, because they never took the initiative to do anything. Ultimately, it's still each person's responsibility to plan for their retirement.

Here is another way to look at it. Let's say your employer matches 50 cents on the dollar up to 6% of your paycheck. That's equivalent to a 50% return on your money the first year. Why would you pass up a 50% return? And if you're not able to put money in now, how on God's green earth do you think you're ever going to retire?

If you don't take advantage of one of these vehicles now, it's going to be more difficult as you get older, especially for you younger people. The government essentially told people who are now under 55 that Social Security and other entitlements will be reduced by the time they're ready for it. There will never be a better time than right now for you to take ownership of your financial future.

REFINANCING LIFE INSURANCE

I think life insurance is improperly named. I think it should be called "love insurance," because most times you buy life insurance because you love someone. So let's remember the true purpose of life insurance. When people approach retirement and are debt free, they often say, "I don't know why I need life insurance." Do you need life insurance in retirement? The answer is yes – and no.

That's because every individual's situation is different. I'm going to give you a few examples, and then I'm also going to suggest that you may want to look at refinancing your life insurance. If your life insurance policy is older than two or three years, and you're in decent health, you ought to have it shopped to see if you can get more bang for your buck. Mortality tables changed in 2000 making rates lower.

Here's an example of why you might want to keep your life insurance into retirement: You have two Social Security checks coming in. One of you dies, and the survivor gets the bigger of the two. But you lose one. What if that puts a financial drain on the surviving spouse? The taxes on your house stay the same. Maintenance on the house will probably go up because that spouse may not be able to do the maintenance. So you might need that life insurance to replace that Social Security check. With our sophisticated financial planning program, we can create a model in which one spouse dies (an expected mortality rate) that will show us if the surviving spouse is going to run out of money.

Consider the case we call "pension maximization." A 58-year-old client wanted to retire at 60. He had a pension, basically an immediate annuity, from the paper mill where he worked. He could get $2,000 a month for just him, or take $1,600 a month so that when he died, his wife would continue to get $1,600. That's a $400 per month difference.

We took the $2000 per month but then used $400 and bought enough life insurance to give his wife, if he died first, this same chunk of money. She could then take that chunk of money and put it into a fixed indexed annuity with an income rider that would give her a $1,600-a-month pension. By setting up the "pension max" they both got $1,600, and now there is a very good chance his kids will get some of his pension too. If they had done nothing, the children would get nothing.

Finally, life insurance can replace an IRA. Most of my IRA, and my wife's IRA, is going to charity: our church, the YMCA, and some other favorite causes. Why am I giving my IRA money to the charities, you might ask? If the IRA money goes to my kids, they'll get somewhere between 50 and 70 cents on the dollar after state and federal taxes. By giving the money to a charity, there are no taxes and the charity gets the entire amount.

A Reverse Mortgage is just what its name implies, it's the 'reverse' of a normal mortgage that you are probably familiar with if you ever borrowed money from a bank to buy a home. That could be called a 'forward' mortgage. You are paying the loan off over some term, 10, 15, 20 or more years. With a Reverse Mortgage you are never going to pay your loan off, in fact, you are doing the reverse and letting the interest just add to the loan.

In my opinion, reverse mortgages should be used only as a last resort in order to improve your financial position. But I have had a number of clients over the years do a reverse mortgage and have given them their lives back.

Let me tell you a story. Bill and Jane whose home was mortgage free, retired after helping their only child through college. Shortly afterwards they needed to do some major home improvements and repairs, new windows and doors, roof, carpeting, kitchen and bath remodels, etc. It didn't take long and the money from their slush fund and savings was gone. They went to their bank and got a conventional or 'forward' mortgage. Then they had some unexpected medical bills not covered by Medicare. They needed to go back to the bank to get more money. Their banker recommended a HELOC (Home Equity Line of Credit) rather than the cost of redoing the conventional forward mortgage. It wasn't long before they had more month than money and they both had to go back to work. Bill, age 68, went back to his old employer and was welcomed back in a part time position. Jane, age 70 went to work at a supermarket bagging groceries. When I visited with them for a review I suggested they talk to a lender that specializes in reverse mortgages. We discussed the aspects, it can be a lengthy process, expenses can be high and the government requires counseling to be sure this is the right thing to do. I also recommended they involve their daughter so she was fully informed. For Bill and Jane this was the best solution. The reverse mortgage paid off the forward mortgage, the HELOC and there was enough for them to enjoy retirement.

Though they are happier and worry less after taking out a reverse mortgage some people are disappointed because they wanted the house to go to their children. If you are insurable you could do an asset replacement. For example, if the home is worth $250,000 and the reverse mortgage is $150,000, you purchase a second to die life insurance policy for $200,000. This will provide tax free money to replace some or all of the loan. At the second death, your children can now sell the home and get the difference between the balance of the reverse mortgage if any and the sale price.

CHAPTER 8

CASE STUDIES

Here are examples of two couples and how we changed their asset allocations and investments.

EXAMPLE 1: LISA AND MIKE SMITH

Lisa and Mike are a couple in their mid-60s. They're nearing retirement, and their portfolio is 60% at risk. Another advice-giver had told them that the 35% in bond exposure wasn't really at risk, but I believe it is. I say that because when I hear people say, "My advisor told me my portfolio was safe. How did I lose 40%?" I want to say, "Well, you really weren't 'safe'—you were only safer than you would have been if you had been in stocks."

I did a full risk exposure and had them fill out my family information sheet, which tells me how they feel about things – how much money they feel they should have at risk, their investment knowledge, and so forth.

Lisa and Mike would like less risk. Together we decide that they want 80% of their money safe. They have 20% in large cap stock funds – perhaps 4 or 5 different large company mutual funds. They have 20% in mid-cap, which is more exposure because mid-sized companies have more exposure to risk. They have 10% in small cap funds and 10% in international funds. And of course, there's the 35% in high-grade corporate bond funds.

So, that allocation looks like this:**

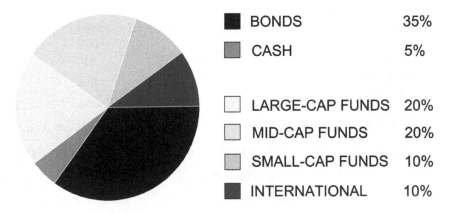

■ BONDS	35%
■ CASH	5%
□ LARGE-CAP FUNDS	20%
▨ MID-CAP FUNDS	20%
▨ SMALL-CAP FUNDS	10%
■ INTERNATIONAL	10%

They did suffer some losses due to the meltdown, and also had a couple of bonds that defaulted, because they had too much exposure to the real estate market. They also have 5% in cash, which is pretty typical.

Since we decided that they want 80% of their money safe, here's what I recommend:

SAFE/NO RISK *

■ INDEXED ANNUITIES	70%
□ INDEXED CDs	10%

HIGH RISK **

▨ MANAGED MONEY MODELS	20%

Based on the claims paying ability of the insurance company.
*** Past performance is no guarantee of future results.*

EXAMPLE 2: MARY AND TOM JONES

Mary and Tom Jones are in their mid-50s. They currently have 75% of their money at risk, but they only want 45% at risk. They own 20% large cap funds, 20% mid-cap, 20% in small cap, 15% international, 25% in bonds and 0 in cash. The reason that they have no assets in cash is because they're 10 years away from retirement. These are only their retirement dollars. They have some cash, $30,000 in CDs and money markets.

So, that allocation looks like this:**

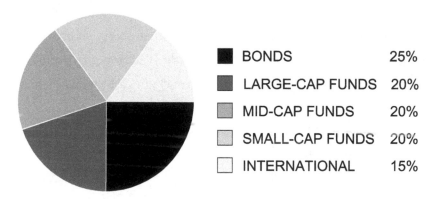

■	BONDS	25%
■	LARGE-CAP FUNDS	20%
☐	MID-CAP FUNDS	20%
☐	SMALL-CAP FUNDS	20%
☐	INTERNATIONAL	15%

Because they only want 45% of their money at rick, here's what I recommend:

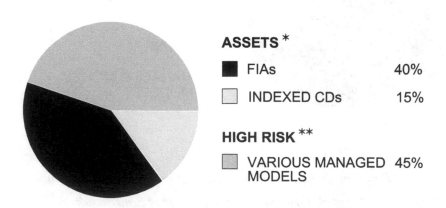

ASSETS *

■	FIAs	40%
☐	INDEXED CDs	15%

HIGH RISK **

☐	VARIOUS MANAGED MODELS	45%

Based on the claims paying ability of the insurance company.
*** Past performance is no guarantee of future results.*

CHAPTER 9

SELECTING A FINANCIAL PLANNER

There are three types of financial planners – captive, career and independent. A *captive* planner is "captive" to a company. If a planner works for New York Life or Northwest Mutual, for example, they generally sell only their products. They have very little opportunity, if any, to go outside their company's products. Brokerage firms like Edward Jones and Merrill Lynch are also fairly captive. Their planners or agents have to work with the products they're given to sell.

A *career* agent has company products to sell, but agents are allowed to sell products outside the box. The Principal Financial Group is a career company, or has career agents.

Independent planners are not tied to any product or company. That's me. I use a spreadsheet and if someone wants term insurance,

I find him or her the best deal. If you want a wide range of choices available to you, then you'll select an independent agent.

Here's an analogy I like: You're in the market for a big-screen TV and you're wondering where you should look for it. You decide to go to Big Box, because they have a great selection, you know their prices are good, and you know they have good service. You're in the store and the salesperson comes over. You tell him that you're looking for a big-screen.

That salesperson's going to ask you a lot of questions: What's your price range? How big a TV are you looking for? Does the room have carpet or hardwood floors? How big is the room? Will you need an extended guarantee or financing? The list goes on and on. Why is he asking you all those things? Because he wants you to get a TV you're happy with. Having assessed your needs, the salesperson pinpoints the right set, walks you over to it and puts his hand on it and says, "Here's the TV for you. It's 36 months, no interest, equal payments, this is such a good time to buy," and then he's quiet. That salesperson is thinking, "I was just down the street at Home Town TV checking the competition two blocks away. They had a better set, better warranty, better price, better picture – everything was better for less money." Now, what is that salesperson supposed to say to you, the consumer, about that TV? If he wants to keep his job, he's not going to say anything. Does that make him a bad person? Absolutely not, not in any way, shape or form. He's simply doing his job. He's working for Big Box. He's selling you the best thing he's got in his product line. It's not his responsibility to steer you to a better deal elsewhere.

That's the difference between an independent agent and a fiduciary, versus a captive or career agent. All but the independents have to sell what's in their box of goodies. They can't go to Home

Town TV. As an independent agent, I can buy it from Big Box, or I can buy that TV from their competition and get you, the consumer, the best deal on the market – and by the way, it's my fiduciary duty to send you to Home Town TV instead.

Here are seven questions the *Wall Street Journal* advises you ask when picking a planner, and my comments on each:

1. What's in the advisor's background? You want someone who has a track record. I don't want to say the more experience the better, but think of your own situation. Do you think you're more qualified to do your job, now that you have a certain number of years of experience? (Or were more qualified, if you're retired.) Only you can decide how much experience you're comfortable with. I don't want to say those new to the industry aren't helpful. We all had to start sometime, and some people take to financial planning right away.

2. What do the advisor's clients say? The advisor should be able to let you talk to some of their clients.

3. How does the advisor get paid? Does he or she get paid by a firm if they sell a product? There are fee-based planners and those who charge a percentage of your assets.

4. Where are the advisor's checks and balances? Does he use any tools in figuring out returns? Does she discuss her plans and products with associates? Does he say it's OK for you to get a second opinion?

5. What's the advisor's track record? Ask for specifics about his track record.

6. Can the advisor put it in writing? You, of course, need a written plan. You need to see what the person is planning for you.

7. What do other pros think? As I said earlier, get a second opinion. Just as I told you to ask someone else about your broker's recommendations. Ask another advisor if you'd like to check on what I'm recommending. No advisor worth their salt will mind, just as a doctor shouldn't mind if you want a second opinion. After all, it's your money, your life, and your retirement.

One thing I say to clients occasionally surprises them: The same person that helped you get *to* retirement is often not the one to help you *through* it. So no matter what stage of life you are in, getting the same advice from the same financial strategist may not work for you. Here's what Michael Gilbert, Chief Executive at Gilbert Advancement, Advanced Asset Management in Kingston, Tennessee, says about why you want to pick the type of planner who will have your best interests at heart:

The problem is the distribution phase of retirement, the time when you withdraw funds from savings makes the accumulation part look like child's play. When you're working, your paycheck allows you to ride out periods of declines in your investments. Once you retire, you can't afford a portfolio or an advisor that asks you to sit patiently through bear markets. If you have depreciating assets, withdrawing money from it could be disastrous.

One of the greatest benefits we bring to our clients is the ability to help them achieve their dreams. This starts with helping them clarify their vision of the future, then helping them make the financial plan that can make that vision real. Your future is too important to trust to the fluctuations of an unsteady stock market or to put into the hands of an advice-giver who doesn't have the expertise and experience you need.

DAVE SAYS...

When you find that trusted fiduciary advice-giver, he or she is going to be doing a lot of what I call "the litmus test." I put the companies I work with through a thorough scrutiny. Even though there are different degrees of "safe" when it comes to money, overall the insurance industry is one of the most solid financial industries in the world and has been for hundreds of years. That said, nobody's too big to fail, as we found out during the last meltdown where we had a major insurance company looking like it could fail. But in fact, it was the banking division of the insurance company, not the insurance division, that put that company in that position.

As I mentioned earlier in the book, there are resources that can be purchased by financial firms which help you assess the fiscal health and stability of a company before you invest. What it does is collect the information from all the major rating services – A.M. Best, S&P, Moody's, Weiss, Street Smart, etc. – and put them all together. Different services have different ratings systems, and what I like about Vital Signs in particular is that it lists them all, leveling them in a standardized format, then gives you what is called a composite rating. A rating of 100 would be the best; I don't know if there's any company that rates 100, but I will only work with companies that have a composite rating of 70 or above. Some exceptions may exist. Basically, the higher that number, the stronger the company's financial rating is. It's up-to-date because it's internet-based, so if that company's rating changed yesterday it's reflected immediately in their assessments.

I speak to hundreds of retirees each year at my workshops. I'm hearing and seeing the same thing over and over, and frankly, it keeps me up at night. I think we all have a vision for retirement. I'd like to share the following letter I received from one of my clients about his retirement vision.

> *I don't have long until I'm retired, and I've been thinking lately about my retirement vision. I'd like to share mine:*
>
> • *I can see myself on the balcony of a cruise ship with my wife walking up to me and handing me a glass of wine…just the two of us watching the sun set over the water.*
>
> • *We don't have grandkids yet, but I can see us doing simple things like spending time with them, teaching them things we've learned in our lives.*
>
> • *I enjoy spending time with friends and family that are important to me, having barbecues, picnics – all the simple things that bring meaning to my life.*
>
> • *I also like to play music and would enjoy doing that a couple times a week with friends.*
>
> *This is how I envision my retirement. But do you know what I don't envision?*

- *Sitting in front of a computer screen six hours a day checking my brokerage accounts.*
- *Turning on CNBC and watching the ticker at the bottom of the screen.*
- *Worrying about money or tracking my gains and losses each and every day. My spouse doesn't picture that, either.*

How much fun and romance will we have in our lives if we worry about those things every day? When I retire, I truly want to retire. Isn't that what we work our whole lives for?

I ask you: do you want to put your retirement plan on autopilot and have a qualified advice-giver manage your money, or do you want to be in the driver's seat? Do you want to be watching the tickers on the bottom of the screen on CNBC? Do you want to be a day-trader in your retirement?

I think I know your answer. You now know how to find the right advice-giver, the pitfalls to watch for and the planning tools you need to use. Now it's time for you to climb out of the pilot's seat and sit comfortably in the co-pilot seat. You still need to pay attention. Don't be a passenger.

HAPPY RETIREMENT ON "AUTO PILOT"!!

www.glisczynskiassociates.com
715-341-8889
800-469-2040

9 781599 322940